Also by Sybil Ferguson

THE DIET CENTER PROGRAM

THE
DIET CENTER

COOKBOOK

by

SYBIL FERGUSON

SIMON AND SCHUSTER * NEW YORK

Published by Simon and Schuster
A Division of Simon & Schuster, Inc.
Simon & Schuster Building
Rockefeller Center
1230 Avenue of the Americas
New York, New York 10020
SIMON AND SCHUSTER and colophon are registered trademarks of
Simon & Schuster, Inc.
Designed by Eve Kirch
Photographs by Simon Metz
Manufactured in the United States of America

1 3 5 7 9 10 8 6 4 2

Library of Congress Cataloging in Publication Data
Ferguson, Sybil.
The Diet Center cookbook.
Includes index.
1. Low-calorie diet—Recipes. 2. Menus. I. Diet
Center. II. Title.
RM222.2.F4269 1986   641.5′635   85-30360
ISBN: 0-671-60445-7

This cookbook is dedicated to the more than four thousand Diet Center counselors who first lost weight themselves at Diet Center, then chose to help others do so.

It is meant to reinforce the principles and ultimate goal of the Diet Center Program: good health and permanent weight control through sound nutrition.

Contents

Photo section follows page 64.

Acknowledgments

Special thanks to all the Diet Center counselors and dieters who submitted the thousands of recipes from which this collection was selected. And to Nana Whalen, who compiled, organized and kitchen-tested every one, to Mary Lee Grisanti, who brought the whole project together, and, of course, to my staff, headed by Jim Liljenquist and Charlene Moore, without whose contributions and help this book could never have been completed.

* PART ONE *

How to Use This Cookbook

Introduction

This cookbook is not just about cooking. After all, cooking is about eating, and eating is about supplying your body with the nutrients it needs to help you accomplish the tasks at hand. This cookbook begins with the basics: good nutrition.

Few of us understand the effects that proper nutrition has on our bodies. Again and again, science has proven the adage: "You are what you eat." Wholesome food, prepared properly, is vital to the maintenance of your mental and physical health— from your moods to your muscles.

Our grandparents understood the importance of eating correctly, on time and on a schedule, to having the energy to work long, laborious hours. Because convenience foods were not available, foods were cooked from scratch only, using basic cooking methods. Our ancestors ate fresh fruit and vegetables in season and then prepared them for winter storage. They drank cool spring water and fresh milk, had fresh eggs, and ate cracked wheat cereal for breakfast.

Today we are experiencing the so-called good life. Foods are available in abundance in all seasons. The luxuries of convenience foods, fast-food restaurants and time-saving cooking equipment have changed the way we eat. As a result, many people are eating foods high in sugar and fat. At the same time, the incidence of obesity is increasing. More than 80 million Americans are now classified as being overweight. In addition, we have become a sedentary society, willing to observe, rather than becoming involved in physically demanding activities. This change in life-style from our grandparents' way has resulted in the obesity that has become a major health problem.

Getting Back to Basics

I have found that nutrition is often the very last thing we think about when we open a cookbook. In part, I believe it is because when we cook we often think about preparing only one meal or one recipe, overlooking the importance of the entire food intake for the day.

Too often, we cook to please, to influence or to win approval from our children, our spouses or our guests. We desire the satisfaction of offering "the best." But too frequently "the best" translates into rich, elaborately prepared foods that almost always are loaded with fats and refined sugar.

Returning to the basics is important to our health. As we prepare food, many of us do not recognize the long-term consequences of our typical meal selections. In this book, I want to convey to you the importance of understanding the basics of good nutrition. Knowing basic nutrition will help you select recipes designed to provide nutritious, beautiful dishes that the entire family can enjoy.

Take time to analyze the foods you serve and eat. The results may awaken you to the need to modify your food choices. Compare the nutrients in a menu typical for many Americans to a maintenance menu patterned after the Diet Center Program (see Table 1). When these menus are compared to the U.S. dietary goals, it is obvious that the typical menu is much higher in fat and lower in carbohydrates than recommended.

TABLE 1

AVERAGE AMERICAN DIET	DIET CENTER MAINTENANCE PROGRAM
Breakfast	*Breakfast*
3 strips bacon	1 egg, scrambled
2 eggs	1 slice whole wheat bread
2 slices white bread toast	butter, ½ teaspoon
butter, 1 tablespoon	½ cantaloupe
jam, 1 tablespoon	1 cup low-fat milk
orange juice, ½ cup	
coffee w/1 teaspoon sugar	
Lunch	*Lunch*
bowl of vegetable soup	3½ ounces shrimp
tuna salad sandwich	½ cup stewed tomatoes
potato chips (1 ounce)	tossed salad (5–7 vegetables)
milk, whole, 8 ounces	Diet Center Salad Dressing
	1 Diet Center bran muffin
	1 cup low-fat milk
	1 large apple
Dinner	*Dinner*
rib roast (7.5 ounces)	3½ ounces chicken breast
baked potato	½ baked potato
sour cream, 2 tablespoons	butter, ½ teaspoon
salad dressing	tossed salad (5–7 vegetables)
dinner rolls	oil (1 teaspoon) and
butter, 3 tablespoons	vinegar dressing
wine, red (6 ounces)	½ cup berries
apple pie	

TABLE 1 (cont.)

	Daily Total for Average American Diet	Daily Total for Diet Center Maintenance Diet
Calories	2905	1400
Protein	119 gr.	96 gr.
Carbohydrate	245 gr.	189 gr.
Fat	161 gr.	35 gr.
Cholesterol	992 mg.	551 mg.
Fiber	4.2 gr.	14 gr.
Sodium	4290 mg.	1444 mg.

	Percentage of Calories Distribution		
	Pro-tein	Carbo-hydrate	Fat
U.S. Dietary Goals	15	55	30
Average American Diet (from the examples shown here)	16	34	50
Diet Center Maintenance Diet	23	52	25

At the Diet Center, we count *nutrients,* not just calories. This concern for total nutrition means choosing foods that are *high* in vitamins, minerals, protein, complex carbohydrates and fiber, yet *low* in fat, cholesterol and sodium. For example, while all meat is an excellent source of complete protein, some choices are much

TABLE 2

	Protein (gr.)	Fat (gr.)	Cal.	% Cal. from Fat
3½ ounces T-bone steak	19	43	469	83
3½ ounces halibut	21	1	100	9
3½ ounces scallops	23	1	112	8
2 hot dogs	10	26	290	80
3½ ounces ham	23	28	348	72
3½ ounces chicken	31	5	173	22
2 slices bologna	5	13	146	73
2 tablespoons peanut butter	8	14	172	73
3½ ounces venison	30	2	146	12
3½ ounces lean round beef	36	9	238	9
3½ ounces hamburger, med. fat	26	18	264	61

lower in fat than others and are consequently better for you. Table 2 compares the different amounts of protein and fat found in an average (3½-ounce) serving of different protein foods.

To provide the body with essential fatty acids, the Food and Nutrition Board of the National Academy of Sciences recommends that children and adults consume 15–25 grams of fat in their daily diet.

* * *

Being knowledgeable about the nutrient content of food is especially important when you're eating meals away from home.

TABLE 3
NUTRITIONAL CONTENT OF SELECTED FAST FOODS

	Carb. (gr.)	Pro. (gr.)	Fat (gr.)	Cal.	% Cal. = Fat	Chol. (mg.)	Sodium (mg.)	Fiber (gr.)
Wendy's								
Dbl Hamburger	34	44	40	670	54	125	980	1.08
Chili	21	19	8	230	31	25	1065	2.30
Frosty	54	9	16	390	37	45	247	-0-
Kentucky Fried Chicken								
Original Recipe Breast	7	16	12	199	54	70	558	0.1
Extra Crispy Breast	14	17	18	286	57	65	564	0.2
McDonald's								
Egg McMuffin	31	19	15	327	41	229	885	0.10
Big Mac	41	26	33	563	53	86	1010	0.59
French Fries	26	3	12	220	49	9	109	0.50
Choc. Shake	66	10	9	383	21	30	300	.29
Filet-o-Fish	37	14	25	432	52	47	781	0.10
Pizza Hut								
Thick, supreme ¼ med.	52	29	18	480	34	24	1000	-0-
Thin, supreme ¼ med.	46	30	26	520	45	44	1500	-0-

SOURCE: The Short Report—Nutrient Values, Health Development Corp., Columbus, Ohio, 1985.

You should choose restaurants that offer many nutritional choices. However, the sugar, fat and sodium content of many foods prepared commercially can be extremely high, generally much higher than even the same foods prepared at home, where you can pay attention to salt, additives and types of oil.

Also, many people are eating their meals at fast-food restaurants to cope with their personal "time crunch." They don't realize that the types of food they eat are contributing to their weight problem. The Fast-Food Nutrient Chart (Table 3) offers a quick reference to the carbohydrate, protein, fat, calorie, cholesterol and sodium content of selected fast foods. These comparisons quickly point out that many favorites are especially high in fat and sodium and low in fiber. Search out eating places that offer fresh vegetables and fruits, salads, and whole grains.

Guidelines for Eating

How do you know if your family is getting all the nutrients they need? One method is to evaluate your daily nutrient intake and compare it to the Recommended Dietary Allowances (RDA). The RDA is a guideline that gives the amount of selected nutrients necessary to meet the daily nutritional needs of healthy individuals. Because the task of calculating daily nutrient intake and comparing it to the RDA can be tedious, other tools are more practical to use.

By learning how to read labels, you can ensure you're receiving the essential nutrients. Food labels use a condensed version of the RDA called the United States Recommended Daily Allowance (U.S. RDA) (see Table 4).

Many labels include nutrition information. The amount of calories, protein, carbohydrates and fat in a serving of the food must be shown. The label must also specify for eight nutrients the percentage of the U.S. RDA each serving provides. Additional

TABLE 4

U.S. RECOMMENDED DAILY ALLOWANCES (U.S. RDA)

Vitamins, Minerals and Protein	Adults and Children 4 or More Years of Age
Vitamin A	5000
Vitamin D	400*
Vitamin E	30
Vitamin C	60
Folic Acid	0.4
Thiamine	1.5
Riboflavin	1.7
Niacin	20
Vitamin B$_6$	2.0
Vitamin B$_{12}$	6.0
Biotin	0.3
Pantothenic Acid	10
Calcium	1.0
Phosphorus	1.0
Iodine	150
Iron	18
Magnesium	400
Copper	2.0
Zinc	15
Protein	45†

*Presence optional for adults and children 4 or more years of age in vitamin and mineral supplements

†If protein efficiency ratio of protein is equal to or better than that of casein, U.S. RDA is 45 gr. for adults, 18 gr. for infants and 20 gr. for children under 4.

NOTE: The suggested daily levels of carbohydrate and fat according to the Food and Nutrition Board, National Academy of Sciences, are carbohydrate, minimum of 50–100 grams; fats, minimum of 15–25 grams.

information on cholesterol, fiber and sodium may also be listed. (A sample label is shown below in Table 5.) Nutrition information is required if a nutritional claim is made about nutrients that have been added to the food.

Most labels also have a list of ingredients showing the predominant ingredient first. The rest of the ingredients are listed in descending order by their weight in the product.

For example, compare these two labels for beef stew:

Label 1: ingredients—potatoes, water, beef, carrots . . .
Label 2: ingredients—beef, potatoes, water, carrots . . .

As you can see, product 2 has more beef than product 1, which means that it would be the better protein buy.

Ingredient labels also list any additives or preservatives contained in the product. It is best to avoid both since we really don't know the long-term accumulative effect on health for humans

---

TABLE 5

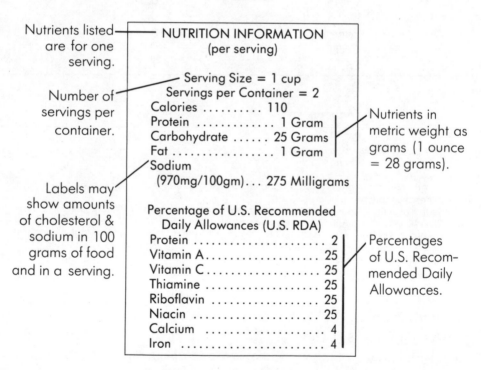

Nutrients listed are for one serving.

Number of servings per container.

Labels may show amounts of cholesterol & sodium in 100 grams of food and in a serving.

NUTRITION INFORMATION
(per serving)

Serving Size = 1 cup
Servings per Container = 2
Calories 110
Protein . . . . 1 Gram
Carbohydrate . . . . . . 25 Grams
Fat . . . . 1 Gram
Sodium
(970mg/100gm) . . . 275 Milligrams

Percentage of U.S. Recommended
Daily Allowances (U.S. RDA)
Protein 2
Vitamin A 25
Vitamin C 25
Thiamine 25
Riboflavin 25
Niacin 25
Calcium 4
Iron 4

Nutrients in metric weight as grams (1 ounce = 28 grams).

Percentages of U.S. Recommended Daily Allowances.

Ingredients: Stoneground whole wheat flour, unbleached wheat flour, safflower oil, honey, crushed wheat, salt, yeast.

who consume small amounts of many additives and preservatives over a long period of time.

Reading labels will help you make wise food selections. You can determine which foods are rich in certain nutrients, thus getting the most from your grocery dollar.

For instance, white bread is enriched with vitamins and minerals and may have the same nutrients as whole wheat bread. However, white bread will not have the bulk and what Diet Center calls "staying power" provided by whole wheat bread, since white bread is lower in fiber (see Table 7, page 29). Many processed foods and fabricated foods (such as potato chips made from cooked potatoes) are enriched with vitamins and minerals. Yet they are not the same food product containing the natural sources of vitamins, minerals and fiber.

In this cookbook a nutrient analysis of each recipe has been given for calories, protein, carbohydrate, fat, cholesterol, fiber and sodium. Check the following section "Know Your Nutrients: The ABCs for a Good Diet" for guidelines on daily acceptable intakes of these nutrients. By eating a variety of foods from the listed food groups, you will be getting a balance of nutrients. You will be able to choose recipes from this book which satisfy your daily nutrient needs and at the same time reduce fat, sugar and sodium for more healthful eating.

Know Your Nutrients: The ABCs for a Good Diet

Whether we want to lose weight or maintain it, our bodies need adequate nutrients to be healthy. Proper food provides those essential nutrients in the form of protein, carbohydrates, fats, vitamins, minerals, water and fiber.

PROTEIN

Protein (amino acids) helps to build, maintain and repair the body. If the body does not receive an adequate supply of carbohydrates or fat, the body cells call on stored protein to provide energy. But if too much protein is consumed, it is stored as fat. Adults and children need only approximately 45 grams a day. There are approximately 7 grams of protein in one ounce of meat or one egg. Therefore, 7 ounces of meat would be necessary to meet the U.S. RDA for protein (7 grams of protein × 7 ounces of meat = 49 grams of protein). Protein is obtained primarily from meats, eggs, legumes, soybean products and dairy products.

CARBOHYDRATES

Carbohydrates (sugars and starches) provide to the body its main source of quick energy. Simple carbohydrates, refined sugars, are absorbed quickly by the body, which can soon leave one feeling hungry. On the other hand, eating complex carbohydrates, like those found in vegetables, whole grains and the fiber in fresh fruits, helps to maintain the blood sugar level because they digest slowly, providing a prolonged, more constant source of energy or staying power.

The daily reducing diet should contain 60 to 100 grams of carbohydrates to prevent the body from going into an emergency situation called ketosis (a condition in which the body's muscles are burned to provide energy). But excessive carbohydrates (those not required for immediate energy) are also stored as fat. Be sure to eat plenty of fresh vegetables. At least ½ of your vegetables should be eaten raw and the others steamed. Eat 3 fresh fruits each day to maintain good health.

FATS

Most dieters believe that because they are trying to lose fat from their body, they should eliminate fat from their diets. But some fat is very important to every person every day. Fat lubricates our skin, helping it to be supple. It protects our internal organs and helps to transport fat-soluble vitamins throughout the body. Natural sources of fat are meats, eggs, dairy products, margarine and vegetable oils. The best polyunsaturated oils are corn, cottonseed, safflower, soybean and sunflower oils.

No more than 35 percent of your total calories should come from fat and a maximum of 30 percent is better. It is wise to consume as many of these fat calories from polyunsaturated fats as possible (see pages 140–41).

VITAMINS

Vitamins regulate the chemical reactions within the body. Each vitamin is essential in converting food to energy and body structure. Because the body cannot manufacture all the required vitamins, it is vital that food supply them. Food cannot work properly without vitamins, and vitamins cannot work properly without food. It is important to maintain a proper balance of vitamins, as either a deficiency or excessive intake of just one vitamin can cause adverse reactions within the body.

Vitamins are generally divided into two groups: water-soluble and fat-soluble. The water-soluble vitamins are vitamin C, thiamine (vitamin B_1), vitamin B_6, niacin, riboflavin (vitamin B_2), pantothenic acid, biotin, folic acid and vitamin B_{12}. The fat-soluble vitamins are vitamins A, D, E and K.

MINERALS

Minerals play an important role in regulating bodily processes. Although the body requires only small doses, they are essential to life. Daily mineral requirements can be met by consuming a variety of wholesome food. Although they are found in the foods we eat, remember they are not foods. A vitamin/mineral supplement alone cannot totally replace food.

Minerals are divided into two groups: seven macro-minerals (see page 122) because they are needed in large amounts, and nine minerals called "trace minerals" because they are needed only in small amounts.

WATER

Water is also essential to weight loss, good health and long-term weight maintenance. Dieters sometimes think drinking water will cause a weight gain. Actually, water helps the body to avoid any excess sodium buildup, which causes water retention. It carries nutrients and impurities from your body. Drink your eight glasses of water every day.

CHOLESTEROL

Cholesterol is a type of fat and an essential chemical manufactured in the body for bile acids, sex hormones and cell membranes. High levels of circulating cholesterol in the blood can lead to the buildup of fatty deposits along the arteries, which increases the likelihood of heart attack or stroke. Dietary cholesterol is found only in foods of animal origin. The American Heart Association recommends a daily cholesterol intake of 300 milligrams or less.

SODIUM

Sodium is an essential nutrient that is found in salt. In fact, sodium makes up 40 percent of the ingredients in salt. One teaspoon of salt contains about 2,300 milligrams of sodium. Sodium regulates the amount of water in the body's cells.

The body loses about 200 milligrams of sodium a day. To be on the safe side, the suggested intake is 1,100 to 3,300 milligrams a day. The average American consumes 2,000 to 7,000 milligrams a day with as much as 10,000 milligrams a day usual for some people. Twenty-five percent of this sodium comes naturally from foods; 25 percent from added table salt and 50 percent from packaged and processed foods. The majority of adults will excrete this excess sodium, provided they drink sufficient water. However, the potential link between sodium and hypertension (high blood pressure) has caused many health professionals to recommend a decrease in sodium intake for all adults.

See Table 6 to find the sodium content of various foods.

FIBER

Fiber, found in fresh fruits and vegetables and in natural whole-grain products, provides the bulk necessary for "staying power." It also aids in proper elimination. A variety of diseases have been associated with a low-fiber intake, especially bowel diseases. Many constipation problems, prevalent among the obese, can be attributed to lack of fiber in the diet. A diet consisting primarily of refined sugars and fat is noticeably devoid of high-fiber foods. Through the years, the American diet has decreased in the amount of fiber it contains.

The term "fiber" is defined as either crude fiber (on food labels) or dietary fiber. The amount of dietary fiber within a given food is usually two to five times as much as crude fiber. Because data on dietary fiber are limited, this cookbook uses crude fiber figures. Most people need to aim for 5–7 grams of crude fiber daily or 30–45 grams of dietary fiber (see Table 7 below).

It is essential to good health to eat a wide variety of fresh fruits and vegetables. For the dieter it is well to remember to eat an apple and a salad containing 5 to 7 vegetables every day.

How to Use This Cookbook

All the recipes in this book may be used in the maintenance phase of the diet. Those followed by (M) may be used only in

TABLE 6
SODIUM CONTENT OF SELECTED FOODS

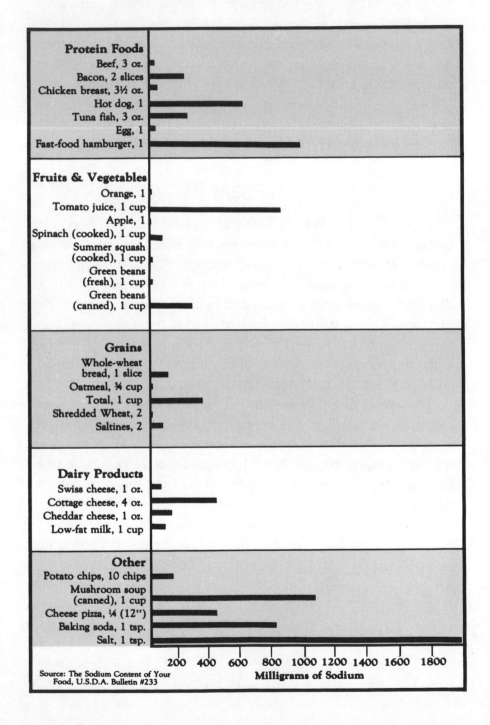

Protein Foods
- Beef, 3 oz.
- Bacon, 2 slices
- Chicken breast, 3½ oz.
- Hot dog, 1
- Tuna fish, 3 oz.
- Egg, 1
- Fast-food hamburger, 1

Fruits & Vegetables
- Orange, 1
- Tomato juice, 1 cup
- Apple, 1
- Spinach (cooked), 1 cup
- Summer squash (cooked), 1 cup
- Green beans (fresh), 1 cup
- Green beans (canned), 1 cup

Grains
- Whole-wheat bread, 1 slice
- Oatmeal, ¾ cup
- Total, 1 cup
- Shredded Wheat, 2
- Saltines, 2

Dairy Products
- Swiss cheese, 1 oz.
- Cottage cheese, 4 oz.
- Cheddar cheese, 1 oz.
- Low-fat milk, 1 cup

Other
- Potato chips, 10 chips
- Mushroom soup (canned), 1 cup
- Cheese pizza, ¼ (12")
- Baking soda, 1 tsp.
- Salt, 1 tsp.

200 400 600 800 1000 1200 1400 1600 1800
Milligrams of Sodium

Source: The Sodium Content of Your Food, U.S.D.A. Bulletin #233

TABLE 7

DIETARY FIBER CONTENT OF SELECTED FOODS

Food (Serving)	Dietary Fiber (gr.)*
All Bran, ⅓ cup	8.9
peas, green, ½ cup	5.4
raspberries, 1 cup	4.6
spinach, raw, 1 cup	3.5
broccoli, ½ cup	3.2
peanuts, ¼ cup	2.9
orange, 1	2.6
carrots, ½ cup	2.3
whole wheat bread, 1 slice	2.1
white bread, 1 slice	0.8

SOURCE: Gilbert A. Leveille, *Nutrients in Foods*, The Nutrition Guild, Cambridge, Mass., 1983.

*An average person needs 30–45 grams of dietary fiber daily.

the maintenance phase. All others may also be used in the reducing phase.

The Diet Center Program is a weight-loss program you can live with. It is designed for people who work and travel and party and play. It is designed for men as well as women, and even for growing children. This cookbook has been designed around complete menus that offer the Diet Center dieter all the nutrients that he or she must have, while still being part of a meal that anyone, dieter and non-dieter alike, can truly enjoy. Complete nutritional information has been supplied with each recipe so that the dieter can choose the correct foods in the correct quantities at each meal.

The following list, Table 8, gives the Diet Center daily food plan to help you choose menus that will provide a properly balanced diet.

TABLE 8

DAILY FOOD PLAN FOR SOUND NUTRITION
AND WEIGHT CONTROL

FOOD GROUP	RECOMMENDATIONS
Protein Foods Poultry, fish, lean meat, eggs, seafood, soy bean products.	At least 2 servings are needed every day. A serving is 3–4 ounces of meat or fish without skin and bone. Provide protein, phosphorus, iron and B vitamins.
Vegetables Asparagus, broccoli, carrots, collards, green beans, kale, lettuce, mustard greens, spinach, tomatoes, turnip greens, brussels sprouts, beets, cauliflower, corn, potatoes, squash, pumpkin, sweet peppers.	Eat at least one cup cooked and 1 cup raw vegetables every day. Have a salad of 5–7 vegetables every day. Dark-green and deep-yellow-orange vegetables are good sources of vitamin A. Vegetables provide vitamins, minerals and fiber.
Fruits Apples, apricots, bananas, cantaloupe, mangos, peaches, pears, grapefruit, lemons, limes, oranges, papayas, strawberries, tangerines, pineapple, blueberries, blackberries, kiwi.	Eat 3 fruits a day, especially fruits high in fiber and water content. Citrus fruits are excellent sources of vitamin C. Fruits provide vitamins, minerals and fiber.
Grains Whole wheat bread, rolls, crackers, cereal and pasta, brown rice.	Eat 2 servings every day of high-fiber grains. Include a serving of whole grain at least three times a week. Provides B vitamins, iron and fiber.
Dairy Products Skim and low-fat milk and yogurt. Low-fat cottage cheese and cheese.	At least two 8-ounce glasses skim or low-fat milk daily, or equivalent calcium content from other dairy products. Provides calcium, riboflavin, protein and sometimes vitamin D.

Oils/Fats
Corn, cottonseed, safflower, sunflower and soybean oils, margarine, butter.

Choose 4 teaspoons of oils/fats daily. Include at least 2 teaspoons of oil.

Beverages
Water, coffee, tea, soft drinks, fruit juices.

Drink at least eight 8-ounce glasses of water daily. Limit the intake of caffeinated drinks to 2 daily.

Seasonings
Herbs, spices, salt.

Season food with herbs and spices whenever possible to limit the intake of salt.

The Diet Center Program:
An Overview

Since its inception in 1971, the Diet Center Program has helped millions of men, women and children to lose weight and to improve the quality of their lives. As a result of the success experienced by these dieters, the Diet Center organization has grown to more than 2,000 locations across the United States and Canada.

The Diet Center Program is both safe and effective. It combines the principles of sound nutrition with the motivation of private, daily counseling by counselors who have themselves successfully lost weight on the Diet Center Program. The program results not just in weight loss but in permanent weight control.

The Diet Center Program is more than just a diet. It is a way of life—helping dieters not only to lose weight successfully but to keep the weight off through a comprehensive education program teaching dieters how to eat. One full year after completion of the Diet Center Program, 51 percent of the Diet Center dieters keep their weight at goal, 64 percent within 5 pounds, and 79 percent within 10 pounds of ideal weight. The national weight maintenance average for people who lose weight and keep it off, using all other methods, is 2–4 percent.

When women take full advantage of the Diet Center Program, they lose an average of 17–25 pounds in just six weeks. Men lose weight even faster, close to one pound a day. This rate of loss can be continued safely until the ideal weight is reached. As a result of Diet Center's nutritionally balanced diet and incorporation of sensible exercise, documented case histories, which include laboratory test results, indicate additional health benefits beyond weight loss. High serum cholesterol, serum triglyceride and blood pressure levels have been lowered. And among diabetic dieters, insulin dosage has been reduced or, in many cases, discontinued by the dieter's physician.

Losing weight, especially substantial weight, is not easy under any circumstances. But it is especially difficult when undertaken alone. The Diet Center counselors play an extremely important role in the program. Dieters receive private counseling and encouragement from these counselors. This individualized attention is a component vital to the dieters' success. Dieters receive not only professional attention but also the care and concern of someone who has successfully overcome a personal weight problem. With the support and direction of a knowledgeable counselor, minor setbacks can be kept in perspective and attention can be focused upon daily progress and long-term goals.

Diet Center counselors are typically not medical doctors; more important, they do not profess to be. They concentrate on maintaining a close working relationship with the dieters' physicians and rely on their recommendations. It is this relationship that makes the Diet Center unique. With supervision from each dieter's personal physician, counselors can adjust the program to meet a dieter's individual health needs.

The Diet Center Program consists of five specific phases, each essential for weight loss and maintenance of ideal weight.

The phases are progressive and are designed to meet the emotional as well as the physical needs of the dieter. These phases are: Conditioning, Reducing, Stabilization, Maintenance and Image One nutrition and behavior classes.

The Diet Center believes that obesity is a disease. Obesity is a recurring illness that is incurable but can be controlled much as diabetes is controlled. We believe that this illness can be kept in check by controlling the blood sugar level in our body. We accomplish this by eating correct foods "on time, on a schedule."

At the Diet Center, the Diet Center Food Supplement is provided to all people dieting on the program. It was designed especially by the Diet Center to help the blood sugar level remain stable. This alleviates hunger and depression and helps the dieter maintain a high-energy level, sleep well and not experience hunger. The Diet Center Supplement is neither an appetite suppressant nor a placebo. Used as directed, it will help you obtain optimal weight loss and a feeling of well-being.

The Diet Center Program is designed to meet the specific needs of men, women and children, needs that are met as counselors work with their dieter and the dieter's doctor.

The Diet Center Program consists of five specific phases:

1. CONDITIONING PHASE

This phase is designed to help the dieter both mentally and physically to move from a very high-calorie diet, rich in refined sugars and flour and high in fats, to a diet consisting of natural fruits, proteins and vegetables.

Two days of a moderate-protein, high-fiber diet helps the new dieter make the transition. It is important to keep the blood sugar stable by eating foods in this order: fruits first, then protein, followed by vegetables, breads and oils. All food is to be consumed before 8:00 P.M. The Diet Center Supplement is taken at 7:30 A.M.; 11:30 A.M.; 3:30 P.M.; and 7:30 P.M. to help maintain the blood sugar level, prevent hunger, increase energy and assist with weight loss.

2. REDUCING PHASE

After completing the conditioning phase the dieter begins the reducing phase of the diet and stays on it as long as necessary to reach his or her goal weight. This phase combines a well-balanced diet of fresh fruits and vegetables, whole grains, polyunsaturated oils and lean meats under the daily supervision of the counselor.

Special attention is given during this phase to appetite satisfaction and basic nutrition. The counselor meets with the dieter six days a week to help the dieter set personal and nutritional goals. She checks on food intake and exercise daily. A weight loss is usually experienced each day and progress is charted.

During the reducing phase the Diet Center Food Supplement is continued to help stabilize the blood sugar. Also, limited vitamin/mineral supplements are used to complement the diet and ensure the daily intake of all essential nutrients. These are 1,000 milligrams of vitamin C and 750 milligrams of calcium. In addition, eight 8-ounce glasses of water and 2 tablespoons of lemon juice are required daily. No alcohol is allowed.

3 and 4. STABILIZATION AND MAINTENANCE PHASES

As the dieter reaches goal weight, the stabilization phase helps the dieter to move from a restricted diet to one that will allow lifelong weight maintenance. New foods are introduced with the supervision of a counselor. Meeting with the dieter twice a week in this phase in private, the counselor reinforces positive behavioral changes. After no longer than three weeks, the dieter then moves on to a maintenance phase or rather a "program for life." At this time, the dieter now eats foods that reflect his or her

life-style and individual preferences. As more foods are introduced, the dieter learns that good foods in amounts adequate
to satisfy hunger can be eaten with no weight gain. In this phase
the dieter meets with a counselor once a week in private to
further reinforce new eating habits. By weighing each day the
dieter has learned to know which foods her body can tolerate
and which foods to avoid. If a person gains weight eating certain
foods, she immediately cuts back the next day to get rid of the
gain.

5. IMAGE ONE PHASE

Image One is a series of video-based classes designed by
the Diet Center to help educate the dieter. Through all phases of
the program, these weekly classes are taught in basic nutrition,
behavior modification, self-direction, stress management and
sensible exercise. The Diet Center deals not only with the physical side of dieting but also with the mental attitude of each dieter.

The Diet Center has achieved amazing results in helping people lose weight and maintain their ideal weight. These results
have been achieved through close adherence to this comprehensive five-phase program.

Staying in Control

By controlling the foods you eat, how you prepare them and
when you eat them, you will have better control over your health
—both mentally and physically. Consistently following these patterns results in a constant blood sugar level, thus alleviating feelings of hunger, mood swings, headaches or an inability to think
clearly. You are able to make positive, healthful choices. You are
in control.

Stabilizing the blood sugar level is the Diet Center's key to
successful dieting and weight maintenance. If you eat a refined

sugar such as a candy bar to satisfy your hunger, your blood sugar quickly rises far above normal. Your body reacts by releasing insulin. Because of the drastic increase in blood sugar, too much insulin is released, causing the blood sugar to drop too fast or too low. As a result, you feel hungry, depressed, irritable, weak or unable to think clearly. In response to these feelings, you may decide to eat something sweet again for "quick energy." Thus the cycle repeats itself.

The consequences of responding to a fluctuating blood sugar by eating sweets can be self-defeating. The body adjusts by storing the excess sugar as fat, and the ability to burn the extra fat for energy is hampered. Both results can cause obesity.

On the Diet Center Program dieters learn that eating a balanced diet of complex carbohydrates (fruits, vegetables and grains) and protein on a schedule, while eliminating refined sugars, stabilizes the blood sugar level. When the blood sugar is under control, more fat can be burned for energy. This leads to rapid weight loss.

Dieters learn how the body responds when Diet Center principles are followed: fresh fruit and vegetables are eaten; fats are not only restricted but all visible fat is trimmed from meat and only polyunsaturated oils are used; whole grains are eaten; all refined sugar and flour is eliminated; and as much as possible, additives and preservatives are avoided.

Dieters and their families learn they have more energy, are less restless and can concentrate better. The body's good health is maintained throughout the weight loss because the diet is nutritionally balanced. And as the dieters learn the physical and mental benefits of eating the right foods, they learn to control their lives.

Are all these changes a result of better diet? I believe they are. Are you interested in these benefits? If so, try an experiment. For the next two weeks, cook everything from scratch. Shop only the outside aisles of the supermarket, where you will find the fresh fruits and vegetables, lean meats, whole grains, cheese, milk and eggs. (You will save a fortune, too.) Avoid processed foods, refined sugar or flour, additives and preservatives. Refined sugar is among the most common additives to the processed and refined foods we eat.

Watch your family's ability to concentrate and notice their increased energy level. I believe you will be surprised. It could be for you the most important two weeks this year.

Make meal preparation easy. Serve a salad with 5–7 different types of vegetables for a wide variety of texture, color, fiber, vitamins and minerals. Broil lean meat and serve steamed vegetables with whole wheat bread. Reduce your intake of salt. Five grams of salt a day is all you need. Most people receive enough sodium even if they never use a salt shaker. Offer a variety of fresh fruits for dessert.

Throughout this book, you will find easy-to-prepare, simple and basic ideas designed to contribute to a more complete and satisfying life. For, ultimately, this is the real message of this book —you can achieve or become whatever you desire through learning how to "stay in control." Learning how to stay in control is what the Diet Center is all about.

Overview

DIET CENTER PROGRAM
Weight-Loss Diet for Women and Men

Daily Food Groups	Phase I Conditioning	Phase II Reducing	Phase III Stabilization	Phase IV Maintenance
Protein Foods	Unlimited servings (10-12 oz. average)	7-9 oz. distributed throughout the day	Unlimited servings (12-14 oz. average)	7-9 oz. distributed throughout the day
Vegetables	Unlimited servings	2 large servings (3 cups raw salad & 1 cup cooked)	2-4 large servings (at least 1 cup raw and 1 cup cooked)	Unlimited raw servings 1 cup cooked
Fruits	5-7 servings	2 large servings	1 large serving	3 servings
Grains	2 servings	2 servings	2 servings	2 servings + cereal 3 times/week
Oils	2 tsp.	2 tsp.	2 tsp.	2 tsp. + 2 tsp. butter/margarine
Diet Center Natural Food Supplement	8 tablets daily	8 tablets daily	–	–
Dairy Products	–	–	1 cup	2 cups
Length of Each Diet Phase	2 days	Until goal weight reached (17-25 lbs. in 6 weeks)	One week for every 2 weeks spent in Reducing Phase up to a maximum of 3 weeks)	One-year monitoring. Lifetime follow-up.
Phase V Image One™ Series	Once a week	Once a week	Once a week	Once a week

A Note on Diet Center Products Used in This Book

The Diet Center Diet has been carefully designed to balance all the nutrients and provide for maximum weight loss. It is a low-fat, moderate-protein, controlled-carbohydrate diet.

A wide variety of products have been developed and produced by the Diet Center to be used in conjunction with the Diet Center Program. These products are specifically designed to enhance and complete the diet.

In this book these Diet Center products are used:

Diet Center Svelte Crackers
Diet Center Protein Powder
Diet Center Lite Sweetener
Diet Center Textured Vegetable Protein
Diet Center Seasonings
Diet Center Crunchies

Sveltes

The breads and crackers recommended by the Diet Center are made from whole grains, which provide fiber. The additional fiber in whole grains keeps the blood sugar lower than does the refined white flour found in other breads. Sveltes are formulated to be lower in fat and sodium than most crackers available on the market. Made from stoneground wheat flour and polyunsaturated oil, they contain 1 gram of fat and 30–75 milligrams of sodium in 6 crackers. This is ⅓ to ½ the amount of sodium and ⅔ the amount of fat in saltines.

Diet Center also recommends Wasa Crisps, which you will find mentioned in some of the recipes that follow.

Protein Powder

Diet Center has formulated a protein powder as a complement to the other proteins in the diet. Two tablespoons (one serving) have 16 grams of protein, 2 grams of carbohydrates, and less than 1 gram of fat. It is a balanced protein product with all amino acids. If you are choosing a substitute protein powder in a health food store, check the protein-to-carbohydrate and protein-to-fat ratios to make sure they are similar to Diet Center's.

Textured Vegetable Protein

TVPs, or Crunchies, are made from soybeans. Like protein powder, they enhance the nutrient value of snacks and the protein value of dishes they are added to. They come in three flavors, ham, chicken and beef.

Diet Center Lite Sweetener

The Diet Center's sweetener is less sweet than most other non-nutritive sweeteners (1 package equals 1 teaspoon of sugar; most other sweeteners equal 2 teaspoons). If you use other sweeteners, instead of Diet Center Lite sweetener, use only half as much as the recipe calls for. Diet Center Lite sweetener contains no corn syrup solids, which can affect the blood sugar level.

All Diet Center products are available at the local Diet Center.

Diet Center Seasonings

A complete line of Diet Center Seasonings is available to enhance the flavor of foods on the Diet Center Program. Commercial equivalents may be substituted.

* PART TWO *

Recipes

Three Important Notes About These Recipes:

Please follow the recipes exactly as written. *Do not make substitutions in the ingredients except where noted.* Substitutions will change the nutritional composition of the recipes.

All the recipes can be used in all phases of the Diet Center dietary program except those recipes labeled "(M)," which can be used only in the Maintenance phase.

Whenever salt is listed as optional in a recipe, the sodium content of the salt is not included in the nutrient analysis of that recipe.

* Spring *

If there is one time of year which is most identified with new life, change and reawakening, it is spring. Those first long warm days do seem to bring a sense of promise. . . . If you are overweight, you long to shed that sad, unhealthy flesh as if it were a worn-out winter coat. You want to be new this year, free and healthy. You want to stop putting off the full enjoyment of life that you know every person is meant to have. You want it to be spring for you in the profoundest sense of the word. And so you make a decision to begin at the beginning.

A Spring Breakfast

Breakfast is probably the most important meal of the day—especially for people with weight problems. Skipping breakfast makes your blood sugar level plunge, which in turn makes you crave sweet, starchy, fattening foods—and leaves you practically helpless to say no. This perpetuates the yo-yo syndrome of starving and stuffing that are the denominator of chronic obesity.

The blood sugar level is the key to weight control—and the key to controlling the blood sugar level is in controlling the types and amounts of carbohydrates we eat and when we eat them.

The basic form to which our body reduces all three types of carbohydrate is glucose. The three types are:

Sugars
Starches
Cellulose, or fiber

All three are necessary for effective nutrition and weight loss. The sugars give energy, the starches—really more complex sugar molecules—carry other nutrients and, along with cellulose, affect digestion to provide *staying power*. This is why it is important to choose natural—unprocessed, unrefined—sources of carbohydrate, whole grains and fresh fruit over candy bars, or cake, for example. The simple sugars in candy disappear into the bloodstream too quickly, overloading the organs that convert them into storable glucose or glycogen. The pancreas excretes insulin to counteract the overload—and the result is that in a little while you want even more sugar. The cellulose in an apple or fiber in a bran muffin slows down the digestion of sugars—you feel fuller, longer.

The following breakfast balances simple and complex carbohydrates and features fruit, fresh and cooked, and whole grains. It is sound nutrition. It is also pretty and delicious, festive enough for a spring breakfast party—a good way to celebrate a warm weekend morning with family or friends. No matter how many guests you have, you'll find that your energy and your spirits won't wear thin. Remember, each dieter must choose *only* the foods that are allowed on his part of the program. All the recipes in this book, unless otherwise indicated, are allowed on the Diet Center Reducing Diet.

*

Special Bran Muffins
Strawberry Muffins
Apple Slaw Salad
Tofu Egg Salad
Sybil's Light Mayonnaise
Chicken Aspic Salad

*

SPECIAL BRAN MUFFINS

1	apple, shredded in food processor
2	zucchini, shredded in food processor
2	eggs
2	teaspoons vanilla extract
1½	teaspoons cinnamon
¼	teaspoon nutmeg
½	teaspoon baking powder
½	teaspoon baking soda
1	teaspoon lemon juice
½	cup Diet Center Protein Powder–Vanilla
1	cup unprocessed bran

Mix well all ingredients except bran in food processor. Add bran and blend briefly. Spoon into muffin tins that have been sprayed with Pam Cooking Spray. Bake at 375° for 20 minutes. Refrigerate or freeze leftover muffins.

10 servings. Each serving equals daily bran and daily protein powder allowances.

Calories	71	Cholesterol	48 mg.
Protein	9 gr.	Fiber	1 gr.
Carbohydrate	9 gr.	Sodium	111 mg.
Fat	1 gr.		

STRAWBERRY MUFFINS

  1 cup strawberries
  ½ cup water
  ⅔ cup nonfat dry milk
  3 eggs
  ½ teaspoon cinnamon
  ¼ teaspoon nutmeg
  ½ teaspoon Diet Center Lite™ sweetener (or ¼ teaspoon of other artificial sweetener)
  2 cups unprocessed bran
  2 teaspoons baking powder

Put the first 6 ingredients in a blender at medium speed. Place sweetener, bran and baking powder in a large bowl. Add batter, mix thoroughly. Spray 16 muffin cups with Pam Cooking Spray, spoon in batter. Bake at 350° for 15–20 minutes.

16 servings. Each serving equals ½ daily bread, bran and milk allowances.

Calories	52	Cholesterol	53 mg.
Protein	4 gr.	Fiber	.7 gr.
Carbohydrate	8 gr.	Sodium	80 mg.
Fat	2 gr.		

APPLE SLAW SALAD

  2 apples (red or golden delicious)
  1 quart finely shredded cabbage
  ¼ cup green pepper, chopped
  2 tablespoons scallion, chopped
  4 teaspoons corn oil
  2 teaspoons apple cider vinegar

Core, peel and cut apples into thin slices. Combine with other vegetables and toss with oil and vinegar.

2 servings. Each serving equals 1 fruit, raw vegetable and daily oil allowances.

Calories	213	Cholesterol	0 —
Protein	3 gr.	Fiber	2.9 gr.
Carbohydrate	32 gr.	Sodium	39 mg.
Fat	9 gr.		

TOFU EGG SALAD

1 pound tofu, grated
3 hard-boiled eggs, grated
7 small scallions, chopped fine
1 cup celery, chopped fine
3 tablespoons Sybil's Light Mayonnaise (see below) thinned
   with 1 tablespoon lemon juice
   Onion powder or garlic powder to taste

Mix all ingredients. Refrigerate for 24 hours to allow flavors to blend.

3 servings. Each serving equals 1 protein portion and daily oil allowance.

Calories	292	Cholesterol	292 mg.
Protein	19 gr.	Fiber	.4 gr.
Carbohydrate	6 gr.	Sodium	172 mg.
Fat	23 gr.		

SYBIL'S LIGHT MAYONNAISE

  1 egg
  2 tablespoons apple cider vinegar
  ⅛ teaspoon dry mustard
  ½ teaspoon salt
     Pepper, garlic powder or onion powder to taste
  ¾ cup corn oil or safflower oil

Place all ingredients except oil in a blender. Blend on high speed, slowly adding oil. Mixture will become very thick. Store in refrigerator, tightly covered; mayonnaise will keep for several weeks. Stir if separation occurs.

1 cup. Each serving of 1 tablespoon equals daily oil allowance.

Calories	96	Cholesterol	17 mg.
Protein	0 —	Fiber	0 —
Carbohydrate	0 —	Sodium	71 mg.
Fat	11 gr.		

CHICKEN ASPIC SALAD

  1 package unflavored gelatin
  ¼ cup cold water
  1 cup chicken broth (boiling)
  5 ounces cooked chicken breasts
  2 hard-boiled eggs
  1 stalk celery
  2 radishes
  2 mushrooms
  1 tablespoon lemon juice
     Few drops soy sauce
     Dash chili powder
  2 tablespoons Sybil's Light Mayonnaise

Dissolve gelatin in cold water. Add chicken stock and let cool. Chop other ingredients, mix and add seasonings. Add mayonnaise to the cooled stock mixture, then add this to the chicken and vegetable mixture. Stir and pour into a mold or loaf pan. Refrigerate at least three hours. Serve cold on a bed of lettuce.

2 servings. Each serving equals 1 protein portion and daily oil allowances.

Calories	303	Cholesterol	352 mg.
Protein	30 gr.	Fiber	.2 gr.
Carbohydrate	3 gr.	Sodium	251 mg.
Fat	19 gr.		

The First Fresh Spring Vegetables

TWO DINNERS

No matter where you live, at the end of the winter there is usually a marked and welcome change in the kinds of fresh vegetables that come to market. Now is a time when diligent shopping really pays off—tender asparagus, new radishes and scallions, crisp dark greens like spinach and romaine, all are bursting with nutrients—and flavor. If you can buy directly from the grower, you're guaranteed the best of both worlds. It's well worth the trouble to travel to a farmer's market or reliable roadside stand. If you live in a city where there are outdoor markets, be suspicious of bargains—sometimes the price means that a fruit or vegetable is too ripe—that is, too old—to be shipped out of the central commercial market. Always judge produce according to firmness, bright color, fresh aroma. Soft, dark, discolored or overly fragrant produce is no bargain nutritionally: it may even be inferior to frozen varieties.

Buy only what you can use fairly quickly. Fresh produce can lose up to 50 percent of its vitamin C as well as other nutrients within *hours* at room temperature. Store in a cool, dry place (the vegetable drawer in your refrigerator can get too humid; if so, line with paper towels)—and *never* soak fresh vegetables in water. Water leaches out vitamins and minerals. Remember this when you're cooking, too. If you are boiling vegetables—even if just to the point of doneness—you are throwing out many of the nutrients with the cooking water. Steaming is always preferable.

*

DINNER 1
Asparagus Roll-ups
Green Apple Salad
Chocolate Orange Cake

*

DINNER 2
Carrot Crisps or Steamed Baby Carrots with Dill (M)
Lemon Herbed Fish
Romaine, or other dark leafy green, with Garlic Vinaigrette Dressing
Lemon Chiffon Pie

*

ASPARAGUS ROLL-UPS

   5   *boneless, skinless chicken breasts*
       Salt and pepper to taste
  20 *asparagus spears*
  ½ *pound fresh mushrooms, sliced*

Pound chicken breasts flat. Season with salt and pepper. Lay four asparagus on each chicken breast, roll up meat and fasten with a toothpick. Place roll-ups in casserole, cover with mushrooms and bake at 350° for 35 minutes.

5 servings. Each serving equals 1 protein and 1 cup cooked vegetable portions.

Calories	195	Cholesterol	85 mg.
Protein	34 gr.	Fiber	1 gr.
Carbohydrate	5 gr.	Sodium	150 mg.
Fat	4 gr.		

GREEN APPLE SALAD

1   *Granny Smith apple, cored and diced*
2   *teaspoons apple cider vinegar*
2   *tablespoons Sybil's Light Mayonnaise (see page 50)*
¼   *teaspoon ground cinnamon*
½   *cucumber, sliced and peeled*
¼   *cup snipped chives*
4   *cups torn lettuce*

Mix vinegar, mayonnaise and cinnamon. Toss the other ingredients in a bowl with dressing until coated.

2 servings. Each serving equals daily raw vegetable and ½ fruit and oil allowances.

Calories	158	Cholesterol	17 mg.
Protein	2 gr.	Fiber	1.4 gr.
Carbohydrate	16 gr.	Sodium	85 mg.
Fat	11 gr.		

CHOCOLATE ORANGE CAKE

  4 eggs
  8 Wasa Crisps, crushed fine (use blender)
  1 tablespoon vanilla extract
1½ teaspoons grated orange peel
  3 tablespoons chocolate extract
  4 packages Diet Center Lite™ sweetener (or 2 packages of
     other artificial sweetener)
 ½ cup water
 ⅔ cup nonfat dry milk
 ¾ teaspoon baking soda

Separate eggs. Beat whites until stiff. Combine all ingredients except egg whites (including egg yolks). Fold in whites by first adding ⅓ whites and then folding rest into lightened mixture. Pour into a 9-inch round cake pan sprayed with Pam Cooking Spray. Bake at 350° for 20–25 minutes.

8 servings. Each serving equals 1 bread and daily milk allowance.

Calories	105	Cholesterol	139 mg.
Protein	7 gr.	Fiber	.1 gr.
Carbohydrate	11 gr.	Sodium	180 mg.
Fat	3 gr.		

* * *

CARROT CRISPS (M)

  1 tablespoon onion, chopped fine
  2 eggs, lightly beaten
  3 cups carrots, grated fine

Mix onion with eggs, then stir into grated carrots. Spray skillet with Pam Cooking Spray. Using ¼-cup measure, make 8 carrot pancakes. Spread them until they are flat. Cook until one side is golden brown and crisp (about four or five minutes), then turn and brown other side.

3 servings. Each serving equals 1 cup cooked vegetables.

Calories	98	Cholesterol	183 mg.
Protein	5 gr.	Fiber	1.1 gr.
Carbohydrate	11 gr.	Sodium	98 mg.
Fat	4 gr.		

STEAMED BABY CARROTS WITH DILL (M)

    1   pound baby carrots
    2   tablespoons fresh dill, chopped

Steam scrubbed (but not peeled) baby carrots and dill in steamer or covered sauce pan (use 1 inch of water) until tender. Serve hot or cold.

4 servings. Each serving equals 1 cup cooked vegetable.

Calories	42	Cholesterol	0 —
Protein	1 gr.	Fiber	10 gr.
Carbohydrate	10 gr.	Sodium	47 mg.
Fat	0 —		

LEMON HERBED FISH

    ¼   cup lemon juice
    ½   teaspoon Italian herb seasoning
    8   ounces uncooked perch or other mild white fish

Bring lemon juice and seasoning to a boil in small, non-stick pan. Reduce heat to simmer, add fish and cook—spooning juices over fish—until fish is done, 5 to 8 minutes. Do not overcook.

2 servings. Each serving equals 1 protein portion.

Calories	132	Cholesterol	58 mg.
Protein	20 gr.	Fiber	0 —
Carbohydrate	3 gr.	Sodium	53 mg.
Fat	4 gr.		

ROMAINE SALAD

1 serving. Each 2-cup serving equals raw vegetable portion.

Calories	39	Cholesterol	0 —
Protein	3 gr.	Fiber	1.1 gr.
Carbohydrate	8 gr.	Sodium	15 mg.
Fat	0 —		

GARLIC VINAIGRETTE DRESSING

    2 large cloves garlic
    1 cup apple cider vinegar
    ½ cup water
       Salt, pepper to taste
    1 tablespoon dry mustard
    ¼ package Diet Center Lite™ sweetener (or other artificial
       sweetener to taste)

Blend all ingredients together. Let stand one hour. Use as much as you like on salad. (You may add 2 teaspoons of oil, per serving, to meet the oil allowance.)

12 servings. Each serving (with oil added) equals the daily oil allowance.

Calories	85	Cholesterol	0 —
Protein	0 —	Fiber	0 —
Carbohydrate	2 gr.	Sodium	0 —
Fat	9 gr.		

LEMON CHIFFON PIE

CRUMB CRUST:
- 2 tablespoons unprocessed bran
- 6 Ak-Mak Crackers, crushed
- 4 Wasa Crisps, crushed
- 1 tablespoon Diet Center Lite™ sweetener
- 1 teaspoon cinnamon
- 1 teaspoon butter extract diluted in 4 tablespoons water

Mix all dry ingredients. Add water 1 tablespoon at a time until mixture is moist enough to stick together. Press into a 9-inch pie plate coated with Pam Cooking Spray. Place crust under broiler for 4 to 5 minutes until lightly browned. Cool.

FILLING:
- 1 package unflavored gelatin
- 3 tablespoons Diet Center Lite™ sweetener divided in half (or 1½ tablespoons other artificial sweetener)
- 1½ cups water mixed with 12 teaspoons nonfat dry milk
- 3 eggs, separated
- ¼ cup fresh lemon juice
- 2 teaspoons grated lemon peel

In a medium saucepan, mix gelatin, ½ sweetener and ½ cup milk mixture. Let stand one minute. Beat remaining milk mixture with egg yolks and stir into gelatin mixture. Stir over low heat until gelatin is dissolved (about 5 minutes). Stir in lemon juice and peel. Pour into large bowl and chill until thick, stirring occasionally. In another bowl, beat egg whites to stiff peaks using remaining sweetener. Fold whites into lemon mixture, pour into crust and chill at least 6 hours or, preferably, overnight.

8 servings. Each serving equals 1 bread and milk allowance.

Calories	84	Cholesterol	92 mg.
Protein	7 gr.	Fiber	.2 gr.
Carbohydrate	9 gr.	Sodium	36 mg.
Fat	2 gr.		

An April Fools' Day Dinner

This is a quick midweek dinner, with your emotional needs in mind just as much as your nutritional ones. Dieting is not just a matter of eating; it is and always will be a major emotional experience, one you want to be aware of and have under your control.

Even the best-motivated dieter has moments when it is really tough to go on. These are the times when you could use some extra help—a word of encouragement from the right person, a little time for yourself and, yes, even a little something sweet. The following menu takes less than a half-hour's preparation. That's time that belongs to no one but you. The baked caramel apples are made with diet cream soda—there's your apple a day plus the old-fashioned taste of vanilla caramel with no extra calories.

And the word of encouragement? The best way to get that is to ask for it. Directly, nicely—you know in your own heart you deserve it. If you recognize and appreciate your achievement as a dieter, others will too. They will take their cue from you. Watch how others change the way they see you when you change the way you see yourself.

*

Fish with Zucchini and Red Pepper
Cauliflower Vinaigrette Alberta
Baked Apples

*

FISH WITH ZUCCHINI AND RED PEPPER

¼ cup celery, minced
½ cup onion, minced
½ cup zucchini, julienned
1 tablespoon parsley
    Pepper to taste
2 tablespoons lemon juice
1 pound fish fillets divided into four servings
1 sweet red pepper, julienned

Combine the first 6 ingredients. Place fish fillets in baking dish, cover with the vegetable mixture and top with pepper strips. Cover with foil. Bake at 350° for 20–25 minutes, or until the fish flakes with a fork. Let stand covered for 3 to 4 minutes before serving.

4 servings. Each serving equals 1 protein portion and ½ cup cooked vegetables.

Calories	240	Cholesterol	62 mg.
Protein	25 gr.	Fiber	.7 gr.
Carbohydrate	5 gr.	Sodium	142 mg.
Fat	13 gr.		

CAULIFLOWER VINAIGRETTE ALBERTA

1   head cauliflower, medium size
1   cup apple cider vinegar
½   cup water
½   teaspoon mustard seed
½   teaspoon celery seed
½   teaspoon dill seed
2   cloves garlic, cut in half
2   packages Diet Center Lite™ sweetener (or 1 package other artificial sweetener)
1   green pepper, chopped
1   red pepper, chopped

Cut up cauliflower. Combine remaining ingredients, and mix with peppers in a large saucepan. Bring to boil. Pour mixture over vegetables and chill 6 hours, stirring occasionally. Remove garlic before serving.

4 servings. Each serving equals 1 raw vegetable portion.

Calories	80	Cholesterol	0 —
Protein	7 gr.	Fiber	2.8 gr.
Carbohydrate	17 gr.	Sodium	34 mg.
Fat	1 gr.		

BAKED APPLES

8   apples, cored
2   tablespoons cinnamon
1   can diet cream or root beer soda

Arrange apples in baking dish, sprinkle with cinnamon. Pour cream or soda over apples and bake at 350° for 30 minutes. Serve warm, cold or partially frozen (terrific!).

8 servings. Each serving equals 1 fruit portion.

Calories	86	Cholesterol	0 —
Protein	0 —	Fiber	1.5 gr.
Carbohydrate	22 gr.	Sodium	0 —
Fat	1 gr.		

Two Uncomplicated Dinners to Enable You to Take Advantage of the Longer Days

The real payoff of your diet is freedom—freedom from illness, from compulsive behavior and from the lack of self esteem that is a true prison to obese people. We have watched the world from behind bars of fat and only dreamed about what it might be like to be thin and healthy, to live life unself-consciously.

Freedom can sometimes seem frightening; after all, being fat used to define the way you dealt with many people and situations; now you have to figure things out in a new way. There's no way around this, so you owe it to yourself to make the most of it.

Now is the time to involve others in your life in ways you might not have before, such as joining a tennis foursome, taking on a new challenge at work, or starting something new like guitar lessons! You'll be surprised how much of your mental space used to be occupied by obsessive, negative thoughts about eating, dieting, *compensating* for not being the person you wanted to be. Maybe you will feel you can direct more attention to your family—or maybe you need to get out and go places you avoided before, like the beach. Relax and let other people get to know the you that has been protected by all that fat. In the process, you will get to know yourself.

*
DINNER 1
Asparagus Soup
Herbed Mustard Chicken
Bibb Lettuce with Onion Dressing
Fresh Raspberries
*
DINNER 2
Chicken Broil
Bean Sprout Salad
Raw Red and Green Pepper Strips
Apple Fluff
*

ASPARAGUS SOUP

  2 tablespoons chopped onion
1½ cups steamed asparagus
 ½ cup steamed green beans
1½ cups Homemade Chicken Stock (see recipe below)
 ¼ teaspoon Diet Center herbal soup seasoning (optional)

Brown onion in skillet sprayed with non-stick vegetable spray. Add other ingredients, and simmer five minutes. Place in blender and blend until smooth.

2 servings. Each serving equals 1 cup cooked vegetable portion.

Calories	39	Cholesterol	0 —
Protein	3 gr.	Fiber	1.1 gr.
Carbohydrate	8 gr.	Sodium	143 mg.
Fat	0 —		

HOMEMADE CHICKEN STOCK

6 chicken breasts, skinned and all visible fat removed
6 stalks celery, including any leaves

1   small onion, peeled and studded with 3 whole cloves
    Several sprigs fresh parsley plus any available stems
8   *peppercorns*
3   *bay leaves*

Place all ingredients in a large pot. Cover with water. Bring to rapid boil. Boil for 5 minutes and skim any debris from the top. Lower heat and gently simmer for 30–40 minutes uncovered until chicken is tender. Add more water, if needed, during the cooking. Remove chicken from the pot. When cool enough to handle, cut chicken from the bones and return bones to the stock pot. (When completely cool, refrigerate the chicken to use in salads, soups, etc.) Continue to simmer the stock for 1 hour. Remove from heat and let cool. Strain the stock into covered container(s) and refrigerate. When all fat has congealed, carefully remove and discard. Stock may be refrigerated up to 1 week or stored in freezer up to 3 months.

HERBED MUSTARD CHICKEN

5   *boneless chicken breasts*
¼   *teaspoon crushed rosemary*
1   *tablespoon Dijon mustard*
    Juice of 1 orange (about ¼ cup)

Sauté chicken breasts 2 minutes on each side in a skillet sprayed with Pam Cooking Spray. Add seasonings and juice, stir, simmer 7 to 10 minutes until meat is cooked through and sauce is thick enough to coat meat.

5 servings. Each serving equals 1 protein portion.

Calories	174	Cholesterol	85 mg.
Protein	31 gr.	Fiber	0.2 gr.
Carbohydrate	2 gr.	Sodium	75 mg.
Fat	4 gr.		

BIBB LETTUCE

1 serving. Each 2-cup serving equals raw vegetable portion.

Calories	10	Cholesterol	0 —
Protein	1 gr.	Fiber	0.4 gr.
Carbohydrate	2 gr.	Sodium	5 mg.
Fat	0 —		

ONION SALAD DRESSING

   1   tablespoon onion flakes
   ¼   cup water
   ½   cup apple cider vinegar
       Pinch of salt
   ½   teaspoon garlic powder
   1   teaspoon lemon juice

Soak onion flakes in water to soften, then mix in remaining ingredients. You may add 2 teaspoons of oil, per serving, to meet the daily oil allowance.

6 servings. Each serving (with oil) equals 1 daily oil allowance.

Calories	87	Cholesterol	0 —
Protein	0 —	Fiber	0.1 gr.
Carbohydrate	2 gr.	Sodium	1 mg.
Fat	9 gr.		

FRESH RASPBERRIES

1 serving. Each serving of 1 cup equals 1 fruit portion.

Calories	70	Cholesterol	0 —
Protein	2 gr.	Fiber	3.7 gr.
Carbohydrate	17 gr.	Sodium	1 mg.
Fat	1 gr.		

* * *

CHICKEN BROIL

  4 *oz. boneless chicken breast*
  1 *tablespoon lemon juice*
  1 *clove garlic, minced*
 ½ *teaspoon poultry seasoning*
    Dash of paprika

Marinate chicken in lemon juice, garlic and poultry seasoning for an hour or longer. Broil chicken five minutes on each side, sprinkling with paprika as you turn it.

1 serving. Each serving equals 1 protein portion.

Calories	177	Cholesterol	85 mg.
Protein	31 gr.	Fiber	0.6 gr.
Carbohydrate	3 gr.	Sodium	75 mg.
Fat	4 gr.		

BEAN SPROUT SALAD

 ½ *pound fresh bean sprouts*
  1 *tablespoon apple cider vinegar*
  1 *tablespoon oil*
  1 *teaspoon soy sauce*
  1 *package Diet Center Lite™ sweetener (or ½ package of other artificial sweetener)*
    Dash salt

Boil 1½ quarts water. Remove from heat and immerse bean sprouts for 45 seconds. Drain and rinse with cold water. Combine dressing ingredients and toss with the sprouts.

3 servings. Each serving equals 1 cup cooked vegetable portion and ½ daily oil allowance.

Calories	66	Cholesterol	0 —
Protein	2 gr.	Fiber	0.8 gr.
Carbohydrate	6 gr.	Sodium	108 mg.
Fat	5 gr.		

RAW RED AND GREEN PEPPER STRIPS

1 serving. Each 1-cup serving equals raw vegetables portion.

Calories	27	Cholesterol	0 —
Protein	1 gr.	Fiber	1.5 gr.
Carbohydrate	6 gr.	Sodium	13 mg.
Fat	0 —		

APPLE FLUFF

6 red Delicious apples
   Lemon juice
2 envelopes unflavored gelatin
   Grated rind of 1 orange
   Cinnamon, nutmeg to taste
   Diet Center Lite™ sweetener (or other artificial sweetener)
   to taste
3 egg whites

Cut ⅛ inch off top of each apple. Scoop out insides, leaving thin shells, and brush inside with lemon juice so that the apples do not turn brown.

Cut up pulp from apples, cook over low heat five minutes, until disintegrated. (Add one or two teaspoons of water if necessary.) Add gelatin and stir until dissolved. Add spices and sweetener and blend in blender until frothy, chill until partially set. Beat egg whites until stiff, fold into apple mixture. Spoon back into apples and top with orange rind.

6 servings. Each serving equals 1 fruit portion.

Calories	99	Cholesterol	0 —
Protein	4 gr.	Fiber	1.2 gr.
Carbohydrate	32 gr.	Sodium	25 mg.
Fat	1 gr.		

A Dinner for Someone Special

Suddenly a certain someone is coming for dinner. Maybe it's your boss, maybe it's an old friend from far away, maybe it's just someone you'd really like to know better. . . . How can you serve a truly special meal and stay on the program?

The essence of successful entertaining is the quality of *attention* which you lavish on your guests. You can serve the most sumptuous meal, the most expensive wine, but if you are always in the kitchen, or exhausted from preparation, your guests will know they have not received the only thing they really came for —the best of *you*. As the founder of the Diet Center, I give many parties. I have little or no time to prepare for them, yet they are moments I greatly look forward to—whether they are business occasions or the rarer get-togethers of old and dear friends. I have three rules for parties that I enjoy as much as my guests.

1. **Prepare in advance.** Shop several days beforehand, except for fresh vegetables, which can be picked up the day before. Make a list. Buy only what is on the list—better yet, look for a market that will shop for you and deliver. This service is common in cities and does not cost as much as you might think. Weigh the cost against the time saved—time you might spend doing something for yourself, like exercise.

2. **Offer food choices.** The bottom line of the menu should be the food you need to stay on your diet. Then, make a few other choices available alongside the basics. You may be surprised, however, to find that many guests prefer the same low-calorie,

nutritious choices that you are making. My beautiful fruit and vegetable plates are always the first to be eaten.

3. *Don't just feed your guests—entertain them.* Take the emphasis off food as the main event. Fill the house with flowers, provide good music—perhaps at a big party, a live ensemble—dress up, dress down, move outdoors. Make it interesting to *be* together, not just to eat together.

*

Steamed Whole Lobster or Split Lobster Tails
with Lemon Butter Dip
Asparagus
Baked Potato (M)
Boston Lettuce with Tangy Basil Dressing
Apricots Ambrosia
Fresh Whole Strawberries

*

STEAMED WHOLE LOBSTER

2   live 1-pound lobsters
4   quarts rapidly boiling water

Plunge live lobsters (head and claws first) into boiling water. Cover and cook for twenty minutes.

2 servings. Each serving equals 1 protein portion.

Calories	109	Cholesterol	96 mg.
Protein	21 gr.	Fiber	0.1 gr.
Carbohydrate	0 —	Sodium	238 mg.
Fat	2 gr.		

SPLIT LOBSTER TAILS

2   six-ounce lobster tails (including shell)
Paprika

Split tails and fillet on top of shell. Sprinkle with paprika. Place in pan with ½ inch of boiling water. Bake at 350° until white (about 20 minutes).

2 servings. Each serving equals 1 protein portion.

Calories	92	Cholesterol	77 mg.
Protein	17 gr.	Fiber	0.1 gr.
Carbohydrate	1 gr.	Sodium	210 mg.
Fat	2 gr.		

LEMON BUTTER DIP

Heat lemon juice with a dash of butter-flavored salt.

ASPARAGUS

1 serving. Each 1-cup serving equals cooked vegetable portion.

Calories	29	Cholesterol	0 —
Protein	3 gr.	Fiber	1 gr.
Carbohydrate	5 gr.	Sodium	173 mg.
Fat	0 —		

BAKED POTATO (M)

1 serving. Each serving equals 1 cooked vegetable portion.

Calories	145	Cholesterol	0 —
Protein	4 gr.	Fiber	0.9 gr.
Carbohydrate	33 gr.	Sodium	190 mg.
Fat	0 —		

BOSTON LETTUCE

1 serving. Each 1½-cup serving equals raw vegetable portion.

Calories	22	Cholesterol	0 —
Protein	1 gr.	Fiber	1.3 gr.
Carbohydrate	5 gr.	Sodium	11 mg.
Fat	0 —		

TANGY BASIL DRESSING

- 2 tablespoons apple cider vinegar
- 2 teaspoons safflower oil
- ¼ teaspoon crushed basil or 6 large fresh basil leaves, chopped
  Salt, pepper to taste

Blend all ingredients in blender or shaker. Store in refrigerator.

1 serving. Each serving equals daily oil allowance.

Calories	86	Cholesterol	0 —
Protein	0 —	Fiber	0.1 gr.
Carbohydrate	2 gr.	Sodium	1 mg.
Fat	9 gr.		

APRICOTS AMBROSIA

2   *cups fresh apricots, halved*
2   *egg whites, beaten stiff with dash of Diet Center Lite™ sweetener (or other artificial sweetener), dash of vanilla extract*

Chop apricots in blender. Drain off excess liquid. Fold egg whites into apricots, spoon into individual glasses and chill. Serve with one or two perfect whole strawberries.

4 servings. Each serving equals ½ fruit portion.

Calories	62	Cholesterol	0 —
Protein	3 gr.	Fiber	.5 gr.
Carbohydrate	12 gr.	Sodium	23 mg.
Fat	1 gr.		

FRESH WHOLE STRAWBERRIES

1 serving. Each serving equals 1 fruit portion.

Calories	45	Cholesterol	0 —
Protein	1 gr.	Fiber	0.7 gr.
Carbohydrate	10 gr.	Sodium	2 mg.
Fat	1 gr.		

An Old-Fashioned Sunday Dinner

Big, traditional family meals can sometimes be stressful events for serious dieters. Your old eating dynamics can come back to haunt you when the whole family is assembled around the table, especially on holidays. Deep-rooted patterns of be-havior—not all positive—automatically go into effect on such occasions. Add that to the stress of staying on a diet and you have a very high potential for aggravation and anxiety.

Although the Diet Center Program is designed for all your needs—first and foremost nutritional ones, so that you are not hungry, exhausted or irritable—the discipline of any diet can be stressful, and not just for you but for the people closest to you as well. One good way to cope with this is to extend to them the techniques of visualization. As practiced at the Diet Center, visualization means taking time out, relaxing and closing your eyes and mentally picturing your thin, healthy body, experiencing the feelings you know you will have when you're thin. Share this vision of health and freedom with your family, involve them in it. Ask them to help you imagine your success—perhaps picture a vacation you might take with someone, camping, skiing or merely visiting places and friends you have been missing out on. Thank them for support and let them know they have a role in your success. Let them know, as well, all that you are learning about nutrition. Meals like the following can satisfy everyone's expectations, and eating right is something everyone can feel proud of.

*

Sunny Citrus Chicken
Green Beans with Mushrooms
Super Slaw
Whole Wheat Biscuits (M) or Wasa Crisps
Apple-Banana Ice Cream (M) or Apple Ice
*

SUNNY CITRUS CHICKEN

  8   *ounces chicken breasts*
 ½   *teaspoon curry powder*
 ¼   *teaspoon garlic powder*

½ teaspoon orange rind
  Juice of 1 orange
2 tablespoons lemon juice

Place chicken breasts in baking dish. Combine remaining ingredients and pour over chicken. Cover and bake at 350° for 30 minutes. Uncover and bake about 10 minutes more, until chicken is tender. May be served on a platter with additional slices of orange and lemon.

2 servings. Each serving equals 1 protein portion.

Calories	174	Cholesterol	85 mg.
Protein	31 gr.	Fiber	0.1 gr.
Carbohydrate	2 gr.	Sodium	75 mg.
Fat	4 gr.		

GREEN BEANS WITH MUSHROOMS

2 tablespoons onion, chopped
¾ pound fresh green beans
½ cup sliced mushrooms
¼ cup Homemade Chicken Stock (see page 62)

In saucepan sprayed with Pam Cooking Spray, sauté onion until translucent. Add green beans, mushrooms and stock. Simmer until beans are tender but crisp.

2 servings. Each serving equals 1 cup cooked vegetable portion.

Calories	46	Cholesterol	0 —
Protein	3 gr.	Fiber	1.8 gr.
Carbohydrate	9 gr.	Sodium	20 mg.
Fat	0 —		

SUPER SLAW

⅔　cup cabbage, shredded
1　cucumber or 1 small zucchini, diced
1½　teaspoons nonfat dry milk
2　tablespoons apple cider vinegar
　　Onion powder to taste
1　tablespoon Sybil's Light Mayonnaise (see page 50)
⅓　cup celery, diced

Mix all ingredients together, chill and serve.

1 serving. Each serving equals raw vegetable portion, daily milk and oil allowances.

Calories	153	Cholesterol	18 mg.
Protein	4 gr.	Fiber	1.4 gr.
Carbohydrate	13 gr.	Sodium	111 mg.
Fat	11 gr.		

WHOLE WHEAT BISCUITS (M)

2　cups whole wheat flour
2　teaspoons baking powder
1　teaspoon baking soda
½　teaspoon salt
⅓　cup safflower oil
⅔　cup buttermilk

Stir dry ingredients together. Pour oil and buttermilk into same measuring cup, then add to dry ingredients. Stir into a ball. If too dry add more buttermilk; if too wet add more flour (consistency depends on the type of whole wheat flour used). Pat out to ½ inch and use biscuit cutter (these do not rise a great deal so do not pat out thinner than ½ inch; you may make the biscuits thicker if desired). Place in a pan sprayed with Pam Cooking Spray. Bake at 450° for approximately 15 minutes.

12 servings. Each serving equals 1 whole wheat allowance.

Calories	142	Cholesterol	1 mg.
Protein	3 gr.	Fiber	0.1 gr.
Carbohydrate	18 gr.	Sodium	224 mg.
Fat	6 gr.		

WASA CRISP FIBER PLUS

2 crackers equal 1 serving. Each serving equals ½ daily bread allowance.

Calories	30	Cholesterol	0 —
Protein	1 gr.	Fiber	2.7 gr.
Carbohydrate	7 gr.	Sodium	20 mg.
Fat	0 —		

APPLE-BANANA ICE CREAM (M)

- 1 apple, diced
- ½ banana
- ⅓ cup non-fat dry milk
- 1 cup skim milk
- 2 packages Diet Center Lite™ sweetener (or 1 package other artificial sweetener) or honey to taste
- 2 drops almond extract

Combine all ingredients in blender. Blend thoroughly, then pour into a covered container and freeze. Thaw slightly and reblend before serving.

2 servings. Each serving equals 1 fruit and 1 milk portion.

Calories	183	Cholesterol	6 mg.
Protein	12 gr.	Fiber	0.7 gr.
Carbohydrate	34 gr.	Sodium	169 mg.
Fat	1 gr.		

APPLE ICE

4 large apples
1 teaspoon lemon juice
Dash of cinnamon

Core, but do not peel, apples and slice into quarters. Cook apples, juice and spice in small saucepan with just enough water to keep from sticking to bottom of pan. When just cooked, cool and place in freezer. Stir every so often to prevent mixture from turning too hard. Serve when still semi-soft.

4 servings. Each serving equals 1 fruit portion.

Calories	175	Cholesterol	0 —
Protein	1 gr.	Fiber	2.9 gr.
Carbohydrate	46 gr.	Sodium	4 mg.
Fat	2 gr.		

Four Salad Dressings for Tender Spring Greens

A crisp green salad of fresh produce is one of the simplest and easiest dishes you can serve. At Diet Center, we encourage clients to have a large raw vegetable salad every day. Use 5 to 7 different vegetables to obtain the best variety of vitamins and other essential nutrients. Contrast is the secret: try a combination of two or more greens for new tastes, exciting textures.

The perfect salad is made with just the right dressing. Go lightly—the dressing should just add sparkle to the leaf, not pool in the bottom of the bowl. All the following dressings are high in flavor and nutrients but low in fat.

*
Tofu Dressing
Green Onion Dressing
Green Goddess Dressing
Egg Salad Dressing
*

TOFU DRESSING

   8   ounces tofu, pressed
   ½   cup cold water (more may be added if needed for proper consistency)
   ¼   cup apple cider vinegar
   1   cucumber, chopped or 1 cup fresh spinach, washed and dried
   6   scallions (including tops), sliced
   3   stalks celery, chopped
       Diet Center Lite™ sweetener (or other artificial sweetener) to taste
   1   clove garlic
       Dill weed
       Pepper to taste

Place the first three ingredients in blender or food processor. Blend until smooth, adding more water if needed. Add remaining ingredients and blend until vegetables are incorporated into the tofu mixture. May be very smooth, or slightly chunky, as you prefer.

4 servings. Each serving equals ¼ protein portion.

Calories	59	Cholesterol	0 —
Protein	5 gr.	Fiber	0.5 gr.
Carbohydrate	6 gr.	Sodium	23 mg.
Fat	3 gr.		

GREEN ONION DRESSING

4   ounces tofu, pressed
5   whole scallions
2   tablespoons apple cider vinegar
2   tablespoons lemon juice
¼   teaspoon black pepper

Blend all ingredients until smooth.

2 servings. Each serving equals ¼ protein portion.

Calories	54	Cholesterol	0 —
Protein	5 gr.	Fiber	0.2 gr.
Carbohydrate	5 gr.	Sodium	5 mg.
Fat	2 gr.		

GREEN GODDESS DRESSING

4   ounces tofu, pressed
¼   cup apple cider vinegar
2   celery stalks
2   raw spinach leaves
8   large sprigs fresh parsley
    Dash each of tarragon, black pepper
1   clove garlic
    Lemon juice or water for processing

Combine first 8 ingredients in blender. Blend until smooth and creamy, adding lemon juice or water as needed.

2 servings. Each serving equals ¼ protein portion.

Calories	58	Cholesterol	0 —
Protein	5 gr.	Fiber	0.4 gr.
Carbohydrate	6 gr.	Sodium	66 mg.
Fat	3 gr.		

EGG SALAD DRESSING

3   hard-cooked eggs
2   tablespoons water
1   tablespoon apple cider vinegar
2   teaspoons lemon juice
    Salt and pepper to taste
    Garlic powder to taste

Put eggs in blender and blend. Add water, vinegar, and lemon juice. Add salt and pepper and garlic powder. Blend until mixture becomes creamy.

6 servings. Each serving equals ¼ protein portion.

Calories	41	Cholesterol	137 mg.
Protein	3 gr.	Fiber	0 —
Carbohydrate	1 gr.	Sodium	35 mg.
Fat	3 gr.		

An Elegant French Lunch

We talked about "visualization" above—the art of closing your eyes, relaxing and seeing yourself in your mind's eye the way you want to be. As you relax, you become aware of yourself and your body in a heightened way; you begin to feel how your health has already improved, how much more alive you are. You picture your face, your body, your hair. You see in your own eyes the special glow that comes not just from health but from self-determination and accomplishment.

This is not just daydreaming. As well as providing a *physical* antidote to stress (as you meditate on your "vision," your heart beat slows, your breathing slows, your muscles, including those of your digestive system, relax and function freely), it also provides an emotional antidote to the poor self-image that always goes with being overweight.

Scientists have learned that one of the ways the brain stores information in its "memory bank" is by images—and it responds the same way to an imaginary one as a real one. If you keep storing an image of yourself as thin, eventually you will feel the confidence that goes with that image. And you will project that positive self toward others.

The following menu is for an elegant French lunch, because one of things people tend to put off when they're overweight is an exciting vacation. But the excitement in life is not something happening on television, or to other people somewhere else. Try to picture yourself in settings you've hardly dared dream about; the person you see really is you—you *can* get there from here by dreaming.

*

Crab Quiche
Endive Salad with Cabbage Salad Dressing
Grapefruit Ice

*

CRAB QUICHE

CRUST:
  2 Wasa Crisps
  1 egg
  1 tablespoon bran

FILLING:

- 1 egg
- 1½ ounces crab meat
- ½ cup cooked mushrooms, sliced
- 1 teaspoon minced parsley
- 1 tablespoon minced onion
- 2 tablespoons skimmed milk
- ⅛ teaspoon dry mustard
- ⅛ teaspoon salt
- Dash pepper
- Dash garlic powder

Soak Wasa Crisps in beaten egg for about 15 minutes or until soft. Add bran and mix. Spray 4½-inch pie tin with Pam Cooking Spray, and press Wasa Crisps mixture in pan and up sides. Beat egg, add crab, mushrooms, parsley, onion, milk and seasonings. Pour into prepared shell and bake at 375° oven for 25 minutes or until just set.

1 serving. Each serving equals 1 protein and ½ cup cooked vegetable portions, and 1 bread and daily milk and ½ daily bran allowances.

Calories	298	Cholesterol	593 mg.
Protein	24 gr.	Fiber	1.2 gr.
Carbohydrate	21 gr.	Sodium	296 mg.
Fat	13 gr.		

ENDIVE SALAD

1 serving. Each 2-cup serving equals raw vegetable portion.

Calories	33	Cholesterol	0 —
Protein	2 gr.	Fiber	1.4 gr.
Carbohydrate	7 gr.	Sodium	17 mg.
Fat	1 gr.		

CABBAGE SALAD DRESSING

1 package Diet Center Lite™ sweetener (or ½ package of other artificial sweetener)
2 cups safflower oil
2 teaspoons dry mustard
½ cup vinegar
2 teaspoons celery seed
1 teaspoon salt (optional)
4 tablespoons grated onion

Mix all ingredients in blender. Mixture should thicken slightly. Keep in refrigerator. Also very good over cooked vegetables.

48 2½ teaspoon servings. Each serving equals daily oil allowance.

Calories	82	Cholesterol	0 —
Protein	0 —	Fiber	0 —
Carbohydrate	0 —	Sodium	0 —
Fat	9 gr.		

GRAPEFRUIT ICE

½ grapefruit, peeled & seeded
Juice of ½ lemon
¼ cup water
2 packages Diet Center Lite™ sweetener (or 1 package of other artificial sweetener)

Combine all ingredients in blender or food processor and blend for 10 seconds. Strain into small shallow dish. Freeze 15 minutes. Stir with fork to break up ice particles. Return to freezer and stir every 15 minutes, until frozen to desired consistency. If mixture becomes solid, remove from freezer and allow to defrost slightly. Scrape into blender and process to desired consistency.

1 serving. Each serving equals ½ fruit portion.

Calories	46	Cholesterol	0 —
Protein	1 gr.	Fiber	0.2 gr.
Carbohydrate	13 gr.	Sodium	1 mg.
Fat	0 —		

Two Spring Seafood Suppers

The object in cooking is to provide the highest-quality nutrition, and the most satisfying flavor, in the least amount of time. With this in mind, you can seldom make a better meal choice than fish, which has the highest protein-to-fat ratio of any protein food, comes in endless delicious varieties, and never takes more than a few minutes to cook.

The flavor of fish depends first and foremost on its freshness. Always try to inspect a whole fish—scales, head and tail on. Is the skin lustrous? Is it firm when you press it? Are the eyes clear, not cloudy? Is the tail normal or dry and shriveled? All these signs are important not only to taste but also to nutritional value. The fish seller can fillet or dress the fish for you once you have made your selection. This is why buying fresh fish in a supermarket, where it is generally already skinned and cut up, is a risk. In such a case, get to know the butcher (a good idea anyway) and always ask when fish has come in.

White fish of the variety included in the Diet Center Program is best baked, broiled or poached with a small amount of liquid for a very short time, depending on the thickness of the cut. The test of doneness is like that of chicken—when cut is the flesh completely opaque, and do the juices run clear and not pink? Cooking times are given here, but there's no substitute for checking the time yourself—and no substitute for tender, fragrant, perfectly cooked fish.

*
DINNER 1
Baked Halibut Supreme
Green Bean Salad Marinade
Strawberry Sherbet
*
DINNER 2
Red Snapper
Lemon-Garlic Asparagus
Apple Crisp
*

BAKED HALIBUT SUPREME

1	pound of halibut
½	cup lemon juice (or ¼ cup each apple cider vinegar and water)
1	tablespoon parsley, finely minced
1	tablespoon scallions, finely minced
	Salt, pepper and paprika to taste
1	Italian breadstick, crushed

Place halibut in a baking dish sprayed with Pam Cooking Spray. Add lemon juice or vinegar and water. Add the minced vegetables and seasonings. Sprinkle with crushed breadstick. Bake in preheated 350° oven about 20 minutes. Do not overcook.

4 servings. Each serving equals 1 protein portion.

Calories	120	Cholesterol	50 mg.
Protein	21 gr.	Fiber	0.3 gr.
Carbohydrate	6 gr.	Sodium	59 mg.
Fat	2 gr.		

GREEN BEAN SALAD MARINADE

3	cups green beans, fresh or frozen
	Dash of pepper
1	teaspoon salt (optional)
3	tablespoons apple cider vinegar
1½	tablespoons corn oil or safflower oil
½	teaspoon chopped parsley

Steam or simmer beans until desired stage of doneness. Drain and turn into shallow serving dish. Refrigerate until well chilled—about 1 hour. Combine the other ingredients in jar with tight-fitting lid. Shake vigorously. Pour over beans. Toss gently, to coat them well. Refrigerate until ready to serve, then toss once more.

3 servings. Each serving equals 1 cup cooked vegetable portion and daily oil allowance.

Calories	90	Cholesterol	0 —
Protein	2 gr.	Fiber	1.3 gr.
Carbohydrate	7 gr.	Sodium	3 mg.
Fat	7 gr.		

STRAWBERRY SHERBET

2	cups frozen unsweetened strawberries
1	tablespoon nonfat dry milk
1½	teaspoons Diet Center Lite™ sweetener (or ¾ teaspoon other artificial sweetener)
1	teaspoon vanilla
2	tablespoons water, or more

Place completely frozen strawberries in blender. Add milk, sweetener and vanilla. With blender running, add water until mixture has the consistency of sherbet. (You may have to stop machine once or twice to scrape down sides of bowl to determine whether proper consistency has been reached.) Serve immediately, or hold in freezer compartment for no longer than 20 minutes; if necessary, reblend just before serving.

2 servings. Each serving equals 1 fruit portion and 1 daily milk allowance.

Calories	58	Cholesterol	1 mg.
Protein	2 gr.	Fiber	0.7 gr.
Carbohydrate	12 gr.	Sodium	21 mg.
Fat	1 gr.		

* * *

RED SNAPPER

    ¼   teaspoon tarragon leaves
    ¼   teaspoon pepper
    2   teaspoons onion, minced
    1   pound red snapper, divided into 4-ounce servings
  6–8   slices of lime

Combine seasonings. Arrange fish in 8x8 baking dish. Sprinkle with seasonings mixture, and top with sliced lime. Cover and bake at 350° for 20 minutes.

4 servings. Each serving equals 1 protein portion.

Calories	111	Cholesterol	62 mg.
Protein	23 gr.	Fiber	0.1 gr.
Carbohydrate	2 gr.	Sodium	76 mg.
Fat	1 gr.		

LEMON-GARLIC ASPARAGUS

    1   pound fresh asparagus spears
    1   medium onion, sliced

 3 cloves garlic, crushed
 1 teaspoon grated lemon rind
 ½ teaspoon thyme
 1 bay leaf
 ½ teaspoon black pepper
 ¼ cup lemon juice
 2 cups Homemade Chicken Stock (see page 62)

Wash asparagus in cold water. Break off tough ends. Combine rest of the ingredients in a saucepan. Cover and simmer 15 minutes, then remove bay leaf. Add asparagus. Liquid should cover; if not, add water or more chicken stock. Cover and simmer just until asparagus is tender.

4 servings. Each serving equals 1 cup cooked vegetable portion.

Calories	42	Cholesterol	0 —
Protein	3 gr.	Fiber	1 gr.
Carbohydrate	9 gr.	Sodium	4 mg.
Fat	0 —		

APPLE CRISP

 1 large apple
 2 teaspoons lemon juice mixed with ½ cup club soda
 2 teaspoons Diet Center Lite™ sweetener or to taste
    Cinnamon to taste
 2 tablespoons Diet Center Protein Powder—Black Walnut
    flavor
 4 Wasa Crisp Diet Lite Rye, finely crumbled

Slice apple and place in pie plate or baking dish. Pour soda and lemon juice mixture over apples. Dust with sweetener, cinnamon, protein powder, and Wasa. Bake at 350° for 35 minutes.

4 servings. Each serving equals ¼ fruit portion and ½ bread and ¼ daily protein powder allowances.

Calories	88	Cholesterol	0 —
Protein	5 gr.	Fiber	0.8 gr.
Carbohydrate	17 gr.	Sodium	21 mg.
Fat	1 gr.		

* Summer *

Summer—sweltering afternoons, ice cream, vacations, kids home from school. In spite of everything that's wonderful about those long days, it can be a hard time to be on a diet. Turning down beer at a ball game, or ice cream on an outing with children, can be trying. Traveling away from home and eating in restaurants requires extra diet-consciousness, and it seems difficult to prepare nutritious meals when it's too hot to stay in the kitchen.

But there's a positive side: summer is the time when the greatest variety of fresh fruits and vegetables is available, and it is the most natural time to get involved in sports and exercise. It's also the time for light, revealing clothing—bathing suits, shorts, sleeveless dresses—in other words: motivation.

The Salad Days

One of the cornerstones of the Diet Center Program is eating on a schedule. This is important, because it is the dangerous dip in blood sugar level—a dip that can come from eating irregularly, as well as from eating the wrong things—that leads to uncontrollable binging.

That means that you must think out meals and snacks in advance—one of the principal reasons we have provided our recipes in various menus. If you are prepared beforehand to put the right choices on the table, you greatly reduce the hazards of shopping when you're hungry and giving in to impulsive, non-nutritive—and expensive—convenience foods. For the most part, foods that are prepared entirely or in part by the manufacturer cannot compete nutritionally with foods made at home. TV dinners—even some of the "lean" varieties—contain more starch, sugar and salt than the same dishes prepared at home. They also contain preservatives and, more important, can never provide vitamins in the same quality and quantity as fresh foods; they are simply processed too much. But that doesn't mean that there are no shortcuts to nutritious meals.

Salads are among the fastest and easiest to prepare of one-dish meals, and in the summer you have the best ingredients readily at hand. You never have to turn on a stove or dirty a pot or pan. With the exception of leafy greens—which should be washed, torn and added at the last moment—most salad preparations can be done a day or more in advance if you store the prepared ingredients properly. "Cool" and "dry" are the words to remember (easy, because in the summer you're thinking that way anyway!). Store cut vegetables in airtight plastic containers, and add a piece of paper towel to absorb excess moisture. Keep on a low shelf of the refrigerator.

*

Crabcumber Salad
Lemonade Chiffon
*

Salmagundi Chef's Salad
Lemon Frappé
*

Red, White and Green Salad
Tofu Strawberry Delight
*

CRABCUMBER SALAD

    7   ounces fresh crabmeat
    3   hard-boiled eggs, shelled
    1   cucumber, thinly sliced and halved
    2   tablespoons lemon juice
    ¼   teaspoon cayenne pepper
        Dash chili powder
    3   tablespoons Sybil's Light Mayonnaise (see page 50)

Combine all ingredients and chill well before serving.

3 servings. Each serving equals 1 protein portion and daily oil allowance.

Calories	240	Cholesterol	357 mg.
Protein	18 gr.	Fiber	0.1 gr.
Carbohydrate	2 gr.	Sodium	279 mg.
Fat	17 gr.		

LEMONADE CHIFFON

    2   cups water
    3   tablespoons lemon juice
        Diet Center Lite™ sweetener (or other artificial sweetener)
        to taste
    2   egg whites, beaten stiff and sweetened with dash of Diet
        Center Lite™ sweetener
    1½ packages gelatin

Boil 1 cup of water. In a small or medium bowl place 1 cup cold water, lemon juice and sweetener with gelatin. Let soften. Add hot water and stir to dissolve. Place in refrigerator until soft set. Whip with electric mixer until almost frothy. Add beaten egg whites and beat on low speed until well mixed. Replace in refrigerator and let set.

4 servings. Each serving equals ½ protein powder allowance. (In this recipe, the egg whites provide a minimal amount of protein, not enough to count against the daily protein allotment.)

Calories	19	Cholesterol	0 —
Protein	4 gr.	Fiber	0 —
Carbohydrate	1 gr.	Sodium	25 mg.
Fat	0 —		

*   *   *

SALMAGUNDI CHEF'S SALAD

SALAD GREENS:

> *Romaine, endive, watercress, etc., to serve 4*

½   *pound chicken, sliced thin & cut in strips*
½   *pound shrimp or crab or mixture of both, crumbled*
4   *hard-boiled eggs*
4   *celery hearts*
4   *green onions*
    Paprika

GREEN GODDESS DRESSING (SEE PAGE 78)

Wash and toss greens and layer on a platter; halve eggs and place around greens, yolk side up. Lay meat and seafood in attractive arrangements, garnish with celery and onions. Sprinkle paprika on eggs. Dress with Green Goddess salad dressing.

4 servings. Each serving equals 1 protein and raw vegetables portion and daily oil allowance.

Calories	270	Cholesterol	322 mg.
Protein	31 gr.	Fiber	1 gr.
Carbohydrate	9 gr.	Sodium	372 mg.
Fat	12 gr.		

LEMON FRAPPÉ

  2 *cans lemon club soda (check for salt-free varieties)*
  ½ *teaspoon grated lemon rind*
  4 *teaspoons skim milk*
     Diet Center Lite™ sweetener (or other artificial sweetener)
     to taste

Pour soda into ice-cube trays. Freeze. Blend frozen cubes and all other ingredients in blender until slush is formed. Pour into glasses and serve.

2 servings. Each serving equals ½ daily soft drink and skim milk allowance.

Calories	3	Cholesterol	0 —
Protein	0 —	Fiber	0 —
Carbohydrate	1 gr.	Sodium	5 —
Fat	0 —		

*   *   *

RED, WHITE AND GREEN SALAD

     1 *small zucchini squash, thinly sliced*
     ½ *cup red cabbage, shredded*
     ½ *green pepper, chopped*
 3 or 4 *fresh spinach leaves, washed and dried*
     ¼ *cup heart of Chinese cabbage, grated*
     ¼ *cup watercress, stems removed (or fresh parsley if*
       watercress isn't available)
       Peel of 1 red apple, diced

Combine all ingredients. Serve with dressing of your choice, or lemon juice plus 2 teaspoons oil.

1 serving. Each serving equals raw vegetable portion and daily oil allowance.

Calories	157	Cholesterol	17 mg.
Protein	5 gr.	Fiber	2.1 gr.
Carbohydrate	13 gr.	Sodium	143 mg.
Fat	11 gr.		

TOFU STRAWBERRY DELIGHT

2 packages unflavored gelatin
8 ounces orange juice, freshly squeezed
8 ounces tofu, pressed
2 teaspoons Diet Center Lite™ sweetener (or 1 teaspoon other artificial sweetener)
1 cup fresh strawberries hulled or 1 cup thawed frozen unsweetened strawberries

Sprinkle gelatin into ½ cup orange juice and dissolve. Heat remaining orange juice to boiling. Remove from heat, stir in gelatin mixture until it is completely melted and clear. Set aside to cool. Blend tofu and sweetener in blender or food processor, add orange juice slowly. Blend on high 1 full minute or till smooth. Stop blender. Add strawberries and blend a few more seconds. Refrigerate in 9x9 pan till set.

4 servings. Each serving equals ¼ protein and ⅓ fruit portion.

Calories	91	Cholesterol	0 —
Protein	8 gr.	Fiber	.3 gr.
Carbohydrate	11 gr.	Sodium	7 mg.
Fat	3 gr.		

A Romantic Anniversary Dinner

Romance is supposed never to go out of style. But for some of us it may have been swept under a carpet of self-doubt and even self-loathing. Your mirror image may have become synon-

"A Spring Breakfast"

"The First Fresh Spring Vegetables"

Red Snapper, Lemon-Garlic Asparagus and Apple Crisp from
"Two Spring Seafood Suppers"

Baked Halibut Supreme, Green Bean Salad Marinade and
Strawberry Sherbet from ''Two Spring Seafood Suppers''

"A Romantic Anniversary Dinner"

"A Child's Party"

Zucchini Quiche, Zucchini Soup and Ratatouille Savannah from
"Five Recipes for Using Up the Summer Zucchini"

"An Autumn Country Sampler"

Cucumber Salad, Mexican Pizza, Deviled Eggs and Cheesecake
with Strawberry Topping from "Picky Eaters, Pizza and Nutrition"

Pasta Salad Primavera from "Three Italian Dinners"

"Some Slimming Thanksgiving Alternatives"

Banana Ice Cream and Orange Sherbet

Persimmon Whip and Persimmon Cookies from "Two Hunt Suppers"

Sandy's Orange Apricot Jam, Diet Center Apple Butter
and Blueberry Sauce

"A New Year's Eve Buffet"

Light Raspberry Bavarian from
"A Midmorning or Midafternoon Tea"

ymous with your self-image. Because of this negative self-image, we often develop external shields—laughing and joking, or hanging back shy—when, inwardly, we long merely to express our own true feelings.

In the past we turned to food for solace and contentment. The kinds of food were typically low in nutritional value and high in refined sugars, which led to blood sugar instability and concomitant depression. And the more depressed we were, the more we overindulged.

But by choosing food, we also did not choose others. We did not share our insecurities—or very much else—with some of the people closest to us. Now is the time to revitalize relationships that you want to give your best to, the way you want to give your best to yourself. You're more capable of it now than ever before —capable of listening to others, of being a good and strong friend.

You've stopped being sorry for yourself and you're glad you're alive. Spread the word; it's inspiring. Show your spouse or loved ones that you care. Say "I love you"—beginning with yourself.

*

Chicken Breasts with Crabmeat Stuffing
Chinese Spinach
Blueberry Soufflé
Amaretto Coffee

*

CHICKEN BREASTS WITH CRABMEAT STUFFING

    4   ounces crabmeat
    1   egg
    2   teaspoons lemon juice
    ¼   teaspoon pepper
    ¼   cup chopped scallions
    1   tablespoon parsley
    4   whole boneless, skinless chicken breasts, about 3 ounces
        each
        Paprika
        Parsley sprigs for garnish

Combine all ingredients except chicken. Spread ½ ounce crab mixture on each chicken breast. Roll like a jelly roll. Place chicken in pan sprayed with Pam Cooking Spray, seam side down. Sprinkle paprika on chicken. Cover with foil. Bake at 350° for 20 to 25 minutes. Garnish with parsley sprigs and more chopped scallions.

4 servings. Each serving equals 1 protein portion.

Calories	208	Cholesterol	173 mg.
Protein	36 gr.	Fiber	0.1 gr.
Carbohydrate	1 gr.	Sodium	134 mg.
Fat	5 gr.		

CHINESE SPINACH

VEGETABLE:
    1   clove garlic, crushed
    1   slice fresh ginger (size of a quarter or add ¼ tsp. powdered
        ginger to sauce)
    1   pound fresh spinach, washed and drained with tough
        portions of stem removed

SAUCE:
- 1 teaspoon apple cider vinegar
- ½ teaspoon soy sauce
- 1½ tablespoons water
- Diet Center Lite™ sweetener to taste

Mix all sauce ingredients and set aside. Spray wok or frying pan with Pam Cooking Spray. Heat. Add garlic and ginger. Stir-fry 10 seconds. Add spinach and stir-fry 1 minute or until wilted. Add sauce mixture, stir and serve.

3 servings. Each serving equals 1 cup cooked vegetable portion.

Calories	41	Cholesterol	0 —
Protein	5 gr.	Fiber	0.9 gr.
Carbohydrate	7 gr.	Sodium	165 mg.
Fat	0.5 gr.		

BLUEBERRY SOUFFLÉ

- 1 cup blueberries
- ⅓ cup water
- Diet Center Lite™ sweetener (or other artificial sweetener) to taste
- 1 teaspoon lemon juice
- 2 egg whites at room temperature

Cook blueberries, water and sweetener over low heat for 10 minutes. Add lemon juice. Pour in blender and purée. Return to saucepan. Beat egg whites until stiff but not dry. Reheat blueberry mixture to boiling. Continue beating egg whites while adding blueberries in a thin stream. Beat several minutes to cool mixture. Spoon into cups or soufflé dishes. Cover and freeze for 2 hours. Let stand at room temperature for 10 minutes before serving.

1 serving. Each serving equals 1 fruit portion.

Calories	111	Cholesterol	0 —
Protein	7 gr.	Fiber	1.9 gr.
Carbohydrate	22 gr.	Sodium	97 mg.
Fat	1 gr.		

AMARETTO COFFEE

1	heaping teaspoon instant decaffeinated coffee
⅛	teaspoon almond extract
	Hot water
1½	teaspoons nonfat dry milk (optional)

Put instant coffee and extract in cup, then add hot water. Nonfat dry milk can be added for a richer flavor.

1 serving. Each serving (with milk) equals daily milk allowance.

Calories	14	Cholesterol	1 mg.
Protein	1 gr.	Fiber	0 —
Carbohydrate	2 gr.	Sodium	21 mg.
Fat	0 —		

A Fourth of July Picnic

Now is the time to get outdoors and move. Not only is the weather perfect, but big family gatherings can be much easier and more fun if they are organized around an activity other than eating.

You probably know that *aerobic* exercise requires oxygen to break down glucose for energy. Regular, sustained and moderately intense aerobic exercise makes your body burn up the fatty acids stored in fatty tissue. This is terrific for weight loss for a number of reasons.

1. You are losing adipose tissue—fat.

2. Your appetite is suppressed.

3. Your lung capacity is expanded, taking in more oxygen from the same amount of air.

4. Your heart doesn't have to work as hard because more oxygen is readily available.

5. Your moods are lifted. We don't know all the chemical reasons why, but one of the benefits of regular aerobic exercise is a positive feeling about life, an increased ability to cope. Psychologists and psychiatrists now often prescribe regimens of walking, running or swimming for depression. And as you know, depression is one of the chief pitfalls for dieters.

So why not incorporate exercise into the annual family outing? Family team sports like softball, volley ball or even just relay races can be wonderful ways to bring people out of themselves. Notice how much more people laugh and smile when they're catching their breath, how much better the food tastes, how much everyone remembers the day. . . . Don't forget to bring a camera!

*

Grilled Fish or Shrimp
Chicken Shish Kebab
Cucumber Salad
Red, White and Green Salad (see page 93)
Apple Cookies
Chewy Oatmeal Fruit Bars (M)

*

GRILLED FISH OR SHRIMP

4   ounces halibut fillet or 4 ounces (4 large) shrimp, unpeeled

Punch seven or so holes in a piece of aluminum foil. Place fish on foil, leaving foil flat. Season with pepper, paprika and lemon.

Place on charcoal or gas grill. Do not wrap foil around fish. Cooks in 5 to 10 minutes; done when the halibut is white, the shrimp pink.

1 serving. Each serving equals 1 protein portion.

Calories	129	Cholesterol	67 mg.
Protein	26 gr.	Fiber	0 —
Carbohydrate	0 —	Sodium	72 mg.
Fat	2 gr.		

CHICKEN SHISH KEBAB

    2   chicken breasts (4 ounces each)
    ½   cup cider vinegar
    1   teaspoon Diet Center Lite™ sweetener (or ½ teaspoon
        other artificial sweetener)
        Dash soy sauce
    2   cups mixed raw vegetables: onion, green pepper or
        zucchini

Cut chicken into 1½-inch cubes. Mix marinade ingredients, pour over chicken and soak for 3 to 4 hours or overnight. Cut vegetables into similar chunks. Thread chicken and vegetables alternately onto 2 skewers, ½ of each onto each skewer. Grill over medium heat until chicken is done and vegetables are tender crisp (10 to 15 minutes).

2 servings. Each serving equals 1 protein and 1 cup cooked vegetable portions.

Calories	224	Cholesterol	0 —
Protein	33 gr.	Fiber	1.5 gr.
Carbohydrate	15 gr.	Sodium	131 mg.
Fat	4 gr.		

CUCUMBER SALAD

3   medium cucumbers, unpeeled and thinly sliced
1   cup apple cider vinegar
1   teaspoon Diet Center Lite™ sweetener (or ½ teaspoon
    other artificial sweetener)
    Salt and pepper to taste
3   tablespoons chopped fresh dill

Put cucumbers into bowl. In a separate bowl, combine remaining ingredients. Pour over cucumbers and mix. Refrigerate.

2 servings. Each serving equals 1 raw vegetable portion.

Calories	66	Cholesterol	0 —
Protein	3 gr.	Fiber	2.1 gr.
Carbohydrate	18 gr.	Sodium	26 mg.
Fat	0 —		

APPLE COOKIES

1   egg, beaten
2   tablespoons Diet Center Protein Powder
1½   teaspoons nonfat dry milk
½   teaspoon Diet Center Lite™ sweetener (or ¼ teaspoon
     other artificial sweetener)
¼   teaspoon baking soda
¼   teaspoon cinnamon
⅛   teaspoon nutmeg
⅛   teaspoon ground cloves
1   teaspoon vanilla
1   apple with peel grated
2   tablespoons unprocessed bran

Combine beaten egg, protein powder, dry milk, sweetener, soda and spices with vanilla. Beat well. Add grated apple and bran.

Drop by teaspoon onto a cookie sheet sprayed with Pam Cooking Spray. Bake at 350° for 12 to 15 minutes.

1 serving. Each serving equals ⅓ protein and 1 fruit portions and daily bran, daily protein powder and daily milk allowance.

Calories	339	Cholesterol	275 mg
Protein	25 gr.	Fiber	3.6 gr.
Carbohydrate	50 gr.	Sodium	297 mg.
Fat	8 gr.		

CHEWY OATMEAL FRUIT BARS (M)

3   cups rolled oats
1   cup whole wheat flour
1   cup apple juice concentrate
¼   teaspoon cinnamon
1   cup raisins
½   teaspoon vanilla extract
1   cup warm water
1   banana, mashed
    Chopped dried fruit if desired

Mix oats, flour, and apple juice in a large bowl until lumps are gone. Stir in cinnamon and raisins. Mix vanilla in the warm water, and add, mixing well. Stir in banana and optional dried fruit. Let stand 15 to 20 minutes. Mix again and pour into non-stick 8-inch square pan. Bake at 325°–350° for 1 hour or until browned.

16 servings. Each serving equals one whole grain allowance.

Calories	131	Cholesterol	0 —
Protein	4 gr.	Fiber	0.4 gr.
Carbohydrate	28 gr.	Sodium	3 mg.
Fat	1 gr.		

A Southwest Fiesta

At the Diet Center, we recommend you eat two servings of meat per day (3–4 ounces each). We don't advocate that you entirely eliminate meat from your diet for some enormously important reasons. First and foremost is that meat is one of the best ways to get "complete protein"—i.e., protein that contains the nine essential amino acids that the body cannot make itself.

Protein performs more vital functions than any other substance in the body. The 21 essential and nonessential amino acids that form proteins are necessary to build and repair body tissue, hemoglobin, enzymes, hormones and antibodies. As well, proteins are responsible for the proper fluid and pH balance of the blood—and it can be used to provide energy for other metabolic activities if there is a shortage of the body's preferred fuels —carbohydrates and fats.

Not all meats, however, are created equal. Some particularly red meats contain much more saturated fat (which can lead to high blood cholesterol levels and ultimately heart disease) and more calories per serving. At the Diet Center, we focus on chicken, fish and seafood, a few forms of very lean muscle and organ meats like beef heart, deer and elk. There is one exception to the red meat/high-fat rule that we include in our diet and that is beef heart. Why? Because the heart is a muscle and to work efficiently it must be lean and free of fat. Beef heart is also very high in vitamins and minerals.

*
Beef Heart Taco Salad
Fiesta Salsa with Wasa Crisp "Tortilla Chips"
Frozen Custard
*

BEEF HEART TACO SALAD

   1   *pound ground beef heart*
   1   *tablespoon chili powder*
   1   *teaspoon ground cumin*
   1   *teaspoon paprika*
   8   *tablespoons onion, chopped*
   2   *tablespoons bell pepper, chopped*
   ½   *teaspoon onion powder*
       Large green salad with at least these vegetables: celery,
       cucumbers, green onions, mushrooms, radishes, alfalfa
       sprouts
   4   *Wasa Crisps, crumbled*

Brown the first 7 ingredients together. When beef heart is cooked, drain off excess fat. Divide into 4 equal portions. Put hot mixture on top of salad with 1 Wasa Crisp crumbled in each salad.

4 servings. Each serving equals 1 protein and raw vegetables portions and ½ bread and daily onion allowance.

Calories	303	Cholesterol	311 mg.
Protein	40 gr.	Fiber	2.4 gr.
Carbohydrate	19 gr.	Sodium	214 mg.
Fat	7 gr.		

FIESTA SALSA WITH WASA CRISP "Tortilla Chips"

   ½   *pound mushrooms*
   1   *red bell pepper*
   1   *green bell pepper*
   5   *stalks celery*
   5   *small green onions*
   2   *cloves fresh garlic*
  1–2 *teaspoons oregano*
  1–2 *teaspoons cumin*

½   tablespoon chili powder
    Dash salt
2   tablespoons lemon juice
2   tablespoons Sybil's Light Mayonnaise (see page 50)
½   cup Homemade Chicken Stock (see page 62)

Slice vegetables in a food processor; remove slicer. Use metal blade to mince fine. Add remaining ingredients. Store in jar in refrigerator; use as dip, with Wasa Crisps lightly dusted with chili and garlic powder.

20 servings. Each serving equals daily onion allowance. (Nutrient analysis does not include Wasa Crisps.)

Calories	19 gr.	Cholesterol	2 mg.
Protein	1 gr.	Fiber	3 gr.
Carbohydrate	2 gr.	Sodium	25 mg.
Fat	1 gr.		

FROZEN CUSTARD

½   cup boiling water
1   package unflavored gelatin
2   packages Diet Center Lite™ sweetener (or 1 package of other artificial sweetener)
1½ teaspoons nonfat dry milk
½   teaspoon flavor extract of choice
4–6 ice cubes, 1 at a time
    Extract suggestions:
    vanilla, sprinkled with nutmeg
    maple
    pineapple, coconut & rum
    vanilla & 1 teaspoon instant decaffeinated coffee

Put water in a blender, turn on and leave running while you add the rest of the ingredients in the order given. Serve immediately. (Use enough of the ice cubes to make mixture thick and ice cold.)

1 serving. Each serving equals daily milk allowance.

Calories	37	Cholesterol	1 mg.
Protein	7 gr.	Fiber	0 —
Carbohydrate	2 gr.	Sodium	26 mg.
Fat	0 —		

Summer Brunches

Eating on a schedule is paramount in keeping the blood sugar level stable. Never skip a meal; never wait until you are ravenous to eat. Eating on a schedule is in many ways the foundation of the control that serious dieters bring to their life.

Whether it's a breakfast or a brunch, these meals can help to start the day nutritionally. In addition, brunches are an easy and delightful way to spend time with family and friends. With brunches there are no hard and fast rules about the foods to be served. You can plan your own creative menus. My favorite brunch menu is:

Baked or Barbecued Trout
Scrambled Eggs or Omelet
Fresh Fruits
Bran Muffins

To grill trout, I fillet and skin the fish and sprinkle with lemon juice, garlic salt and pepper. Spray the grill with Pam and grill flesh-down until brown and flaky. Serve buffet-style indoors or outdoors.

Use a large crystal bowl of melon balls and other fresh fruit sliced and diced to create a lovely centerpiece for your table. Eggs prepared in your favorite way, along with nutritious muffins, will provide a satisfying meal.

We're offering recipes for a quick breakfast, or they can be used as a basis around which you can build your own interesting brunch menus.

*
French Toast
Blueberry Sauce
*
Cinnamon Toast
Fluffy Omelet
*
Apple Pancakes
*
Wake Up and Live (M)
*
Creamy Coffee Cooler (M)
Carrot-Bran Muffins (M)
*

FRENCH TOAST

1	egg
1–2	tablespoons water
	Dash of cinnamon
1	package Diet Center Lite™ sweetener (or ½ package other artificial sweetener)
2	Wasa Crisps Diet Lite Rye

The night before, beat egg, water, cinnamon and Diet Center Lite sweetener together. Place Wasa Crisps Diet Lite Rye slices in a shallow dish. Pour egg mixture over, making sure Wasa is completely covered. Soak overnight, covered, in refrigerator. The next morning spray pan with Pam Cooking Spray, then cook Wasas until browned and cooked through.

1 serving. Each serving equals ⅓ protein portion and 1 bread allowance.

Calories	139	Cholesterol	275 mg.
Protein	8 gr.	Fiber	0.3 gr.
Carbohydrate	13 gr.	Sodium	109 mg.
Fat	6 gr.		

BLUEBERRY SAUCE

    1   cup blueberries
    ⅓   cup water
    2   tablespoons lemon juice
    1   teaspoon Diet Center Lite™ sweetener (or ½ teaspoon
        other artificial sweetener)
        Cinnamon to taste
        Nutmeg to taste

Place blueberries, water and lemon juice in saucepan. Cook over medium heat, stirring constantly. Add sweetener, cinnamon and nutmeg. Keep stirring until sauce comes to a low boil. The longer it cooks, the thicker it becomes. Serve sauce on Wasa Crisp, bran muffins or tofu.

1 serving. Each serving equals 1 fruit portion.

Calories	97	Cholesterol	0 —
Protein	1 gr.	Fiber	2.2 gr.
Carbohydrate	25 gr.	Sodium	10 mg.
Fat	1 gr.		

* * *

CINNAMON TOAST

    2   Wasa Crisps Fiber Plus
        Water
        Cinnamon
        Diet Center Lite™ sweetener (or other artificial sweetener)
        to taste

Run water over Wasa Crisps. Sprinkle one side with cinnamon and sweetener. Place in broiler. Broil till sweetener browns. Watch closely.

1 serving. Each serving equals 1 bread allowance.

Calories	63.9	Cholesterol	0 —
Protein	3 gr.	Fiber	5.7 gr.
Carbohydrate	11 gr.	Sodium	0 —
Fat	1 gr.		

FLUFFY OMELET

2   eggs, room temperature
    Dash of salt
    Dash of white pepper
    Dash of nutmeg
1   tablespoon water
8   asparagus spears, steamed till just tender
1   tablespoon Diet Center Ham Crunchies (optional)

Preheat oven to 350°.

Separate eggs. Combine egg whites and salt. Beat till whites stand in peaks. Combine egg yolks, pepper, nutmeg and water. Beat till yolks are lemon-colored and thick. Fold yolk mixture into whites. Heat 10-inch cast-iron skillet over low heat. Spray with Pam Cooking Spray. Pour egg mixture into skillet, cook for about 5 minutes. Place skillet in pre-heated oven for 3 to 5 minutes. Test with table knife in center; when it comes out clean, omelet is done. Turn out onto a plate. Lay asparagus on half of the omelet, sprinkle with crunchies, and then fold in half.

2 servings. Each serving equals ⅓ protein and ½ cup cooked vegetables portions.

Calories	93	Cholesterol	275 mg.
Protein	7 gr.	Fiber	.5 gr.
Carbohydrate	3 gr.	Sodium	141 mg.
Fat	6 gr.		

* * *

APPLE PANCAKES

2   eggs, beaten
1   tablespoon Diet Center Protein Powder, Vanilla or Black
    Walnut
2   tablespoons bran
    Dash of cinnamon and/or nutmeg
¼   teaspoon pure vanilla extract (or almond extract)
    Dash of Diet Center Lite™ sweetener (or other artificial
    sweetener)
1   apple, cored

Mix eggs, protein powder, cinnamon, nutmeg, vanilla and sweetener in blender. Add apple and blend until chopped fine. Pour into bowl, add bran and let sit several seconds. Spray non-stick skillet with Pam Cooking Spray. Pour mixture on preheated skillet to make 4 pancakes. Cook as regular pancakes.

1 serving. Each serving equals ⅔ protein and 1 fruit portions; daily protein powder and bran allowance.

Calories	374	Cholesterol	549 mg.
Protein	22 gr.	Fiber	3.8 gr.
Carbohydrate	49 gr.	Sodium	142 mg.
Fat	13 gr.		

* * *

WAKE UP AND LIVE (M)

1   cup strawberries
1   egg
2   tablespoons Diet Center Protein Powder, Vanilla
1   tablespoon brewer's yeast
½   banana
1   teaspoon vanilla
1   cup skim milk

2 packages *Diet Center Lite™ sweetener (or 1 package other artificial sweetener) (optional)*
4 *ice cubes*

Whirl all ingredients together in a blender and enjoy! This is a great energizer and fills you up for hours.

1 serving. Each serving equals ⅓ protein and 1½ fruit portions and milk allowance.

Calories	357	Cholesterol	279 mg.
Protein	35 gr.	Fiber	1.2 gr.
Carbohydrate	41 gr.	Sodium	207 mg
Fat	7 gr.		

*   *   *

CREAMY COFFEE COOLER (M)

1 *cup skim milk*
1 *teaspoon decaffeinated instant coffee*
½–1 *package Diet Center Lite™ sweetener (or ¼–½ other artificial sweetener)*
¼ *teaspoon vanilla*
4 *ice cubes*

Put milk, coffee, Diet Center Lite sweetener and vanilla into blender. Blend. Add ice slowly until mixture is thick and frothy.

2 servings. Each serving equals ½ milk allowance.

Calories	43	Cholesterol	2 mg.
Protein	4 gr.	Fiber	0 —
Carbohydrate	6 gr.	Sodium	63 mg.
Fat	0 —		

CARROT-BRAN MUFFINS (M)

    2   cups carrots, grated
    1½ cup unprocessed bran
    4   eggs, beaten
    1   tablespoon Diet Center Lite™ sweetener (or ½
        tablespoon other artificial sweetener)
    1   teaspoon cinnamon
    ¼   teaspoon nutmeg
    ½   cup unsweetened applesauce or ½ cup blueberries

Combine all ingredients. Mix well. Pour into muffin cups sprayed with Pam Cooking Spray. Bake at 350° for 35 minutes. Refrigerate or freeze leftover muffins.

18 servings. Each serving equals ½ bread allowance.

Calories	36	Cholesterol	61 mg.
Protein	2 gr.	Fiber	0.6 gr.
Carbohydrate	5 gr.	Sodium	23 mg.
Fat	2 gr.		

A Child's Party

Overweight children can face many of the same problems that adults face, plus some special ones.

Physically, the obese child is carrying around extra weight at the time that his bones and muscles are developing, and his bones and muscles can become denser than normal in order to compensate. Later in life, it will be harder for such individuals to lose weight and keep it off—harder to diet, harder to exercise, harder to achieve the slim and healthy good looks that teenagers prize.

Children and teenagers suffer especially from the lack of a positive self-image that goes with obesity. This is the time when they seek and form their identities. Societal and peer pressure is agonizing; desire for parental approval can be countereffective since parents may be partly responsible for the child's bad eating habits. And a poor image now may be hard to change later.

Parents are responsible for their children's nutrition. It's a mistake to think that because they're growing so fast, kids can't get fat on foods you know are bad nutrition. A child may not gain weight immediately on after-school cupcakes and soda, but he is developing a very bad habit, one that may haunt him later. Do not keep junk food in the house. Try the "take-away system" for enticing children to eat fruit and other nutritious snacks. Keep the fruit and special snacks in the back of the refrigerator or high on a shelf. Explain to the kids that they cannot have them—they might waste them. When the kids think they're getting your special snacks, they'll beg for them. *Never use food as a reward or lack of it as a punishment.* Your message equates care with eating, an unhappy pitfall that most obese adults find they have succumbed to.

*
Chicken Nuggets
Cole Slaw
Popsicles
Diet Vanilla Milk Shake
*

CHICKEN NUGGETS

  2 *chicken breasts (4 ounces each)*
  1 *egg*
  4 *tablespoons Diet Center Chicken Crunchies or 4*
     tablespoons Wasa crumbs
  ½ *teaspoon poultry seasoning*
  1 *tablespoon chopped parsley*

Cut chicken breasts in bite-size pieces, approximately 1 inch by 1 inch. With rolling pin crush Diet Center Crunchies. Beat egg, add spice and parsley. Dip chicken pieces in egg and roll in crunchies. Place on a Pam-sprayed baking pan, and bake at 350° for 30 minutes, turning once.

2 servings. Each serving equals 1 protein portion and daily Crunchie allowance or ½ bread if Wasa is used.

Calories	240	Cholesterol	222 mg.
Protein	40 gr.	Fiber	0 —
Carbohydrate	4 gr.	Sodium	235 mg.
Fat	6 gr.		

COLE SLAW

- ½ head cabbage
- ¼ teaspoon salt
- ¼ cup celery, diced
- ½ green pepper, diced
- 1 package Diet Center Lite™ sweetener (or ½ package other artificial sweetener)
- ⅓ cup water
- ⅓ cup apple cider vinegar

Shred cabbage into a bowl and sprinkle with salt. Let stand for 30 minutes. Add celery and green pepper. Sprinkle with sweetener. Combine water and vinegar, then pour over cabbage. Best after 24 hours in the refrigerator.

2 servings. Each serving equals a raw vegetable portion.

Calories	28	Cholesterol	0 —
Protein	1 gr.	Fiber	0.9 gr.
Carbohydrate	7 gr.	Sodium	313 mg.
Fat	0 —		

POPSICLES

1½ cups club soda
1 package unflavored gelatin
4 packages Diet Center Lite™ sweetener
1 tablespoon lemon juice
1 fruit, puréed

Pour ¾ cup soda into dish containing gelatin and sweetener. Let stand until soft. Boil remaining soda and pour over gelatin mixture. Stir to completely dissolve. Add lemon juice and puréed fruit. Stir well. Pour into 5-ounce Dixie cups. Place in freezer and when partially set add wooden ice cream sticks. Freeze until firm. Remove from freezer 5 minutes before serving.

7 servings. Each serving equals ⅐ fruit portion.

Calories	13	Cholesterol	0 —
Protein	1 gr.	Fiber	0.1 gr.
Carbohydrate	2 gr.	Sodium	1 mg.
Fat	0 —		

DIET VANILLA MILK SHAKE

2 tablespoons Diet Center Protein Powder
2 tablespoons skim milk
5 ice cubes in a cup, filled to 1 cup level with water
1 package Diet Center Lite™ sweetener (or ½ package
  other artificial sweetener)
½ teaspoon vanilla

Blend all ingredients in a blender until thick.

1 serving. Each serving equals daily protein powder and daily milk allowance.

Calories	80	Cholesterol	0 —
Protein	17 gr.	Fiber	0 —
Carbohydrate	3 gr.	Sodium	15 mg.
Fat	0 —		

Three Midsummer One-Dish Meals

One of the keys to dieting success is preparation—having the right foods ready at the right time. Shopping in advance, when you are not hungry, and choosing menus that keep you out of the kitchen—like those below, and indeed all the Diet Center menus—are two good ways of preparing a one-dish meal.

But there is another sort of preparation involved in dieting—mental preparation. The decision to diet, really the decision to be healthy, is not a quick decision that one makes once and is over with. It is a commitment, and like any other serious commitment, whether a marriage or a career, it must be reconsidered and reaffirmed as you go along.

Take a few minutes each day to take account of your success. Reward yourself for your hard work by telling yourself that you'll never let that work be for nought. This is the last diet you're going to be on. Nothing is more important. Put a sign on your bathroom scale and on your refrigerator door: "I won't stop until I reach my goal."

Remind yourself that *you* are the reason you are dieting. It is your decision and your responsibility—if part of your initial motivation came from someone else's prodding, or the desire to win someone else's affection or approval, now is the time to reorient your goal to becoming the best that you can be, regardless of any other person. You're going to lose the weight you have to lose; you don't know the word "failure." This is your chance to shine.

*
Chicken Rollatine
Iced Strawberry Crème
*
Chicken and Green Chili
Honeydew Ice
*
Pepper Pie
Peach "Ice Cream"
*

CHICKEN ROLLATINE

2 cups chopped cooked spinach
2 cups chopped mushrooms
8 tablespoons onions, diced
3 cloves garlic, minced
4 skinned and boned chicken breasts (4 ounces each),
   pounded to ¼-inch thickness
   Salt and pepper to taste
   Paprika to taste
   Fresh parsley, chopped

In skillet sprayed with Pam Cooking Spray, sauté mushrooms, onion and garlic. Add drained spinach to mixture, sauté 2 minutes. Put 2 heaping tablespoons on chicken breast, roll and skewer. Sprinkle with salt, pepper and paprika. In another sprayed skillet brown chicken rollatine over high heat. Put remaining spinach mixture on the bottom of a sprayed baking dish. Place chicken pieces over spinach with chopped parsley, cover with foil. Bake at 350° for 30 minutes.

4 servings. Each serving equals 1 protein portion and 1 cup cooked vegetable portion.

Calories	219	Cholesterol	85 mg.
Protein	37 gr.	Fiber	1.3 gr.
Carbohydrate	9 gr.	Sodium	181 mg.
Fat	4 gr.		

ICED STRAWBERRY CRÈME

1   cup frozen unsweetened strawberries (it's best to freeze
    fresh ones)
1½ teaspoon nonfat dry milk
    Diet Center Lite™ sweetener (or other artificial sweetener)
    to taste
    Cold water to give mixture the consistency of ice cream

Chop frozen strawberries in food processor. Change blade to mixer and add remaining ingredients. Serve.

1 serving. Each serving equals 1 fruit portion and daily milk allowance.

Calories	58	Cholesterol	1 mg.
Protein	2 gr.	Fiber	0.7 gr.
Carbohydrate	12 gr.	Sodium	21 mg.
Fat	1 gr.		

*   *   *

CHICKEN AND GREEN CHILI

1   clove garlic, cut in half
2   teaspoons onion, diced
1   chicken breast (4 ounces), ground or cut into small pieces
    Dash of cumin
1   cup green chili, chopped
1   teaspoon oil

In non-stick skillet, sauté garlic until brown; remove. Cook onion until tender and add chicken breast. Sauté until almost done.

Add cumin and green chili and cook a few minutes longer. Remove from burner and add oil.

1 serving. Each serving equals 1 protein and 1 cooked vegetable portions and ½ daily oil allowance.

Calories	252	Cholesterol	85 mg.
Protein	33 gr.	Fiber	2.5 gr.
Carbohydrate	13 gr.	Sodium	135 mg
Fat	8 gr.		

HONEYDEW ICE

- 1 teaspoon unflavored gelatin
- 2 tablespoons water
- 4 cups honeydew melon, cubed
- 2 tablespoons lime or lemon juice
- 1–2 packages Diet Center Lite™ sweetener (or ½–1 package other artificial sweetener) (optional)

In a 1-cup glass measure, soften gelatin in water. Place in pan of water and heat. Stir gelatin until dissolved. In blender combine 1 cup honeydew melon cubes, juice, sweetener and gelatin mixture. Cover and blend until smooth. Add remaining honeydew melon cubes and blend until smooth. Pour into 8 × 8 × 2 pan and freeze until almost firm. Remove and beat with a mixer in a large chilled bowl until smooth. Return to pan and freeze until firm. To serve let stand 15–20 minutes at room temperature. Scrape surface and spoon into individual serving dishes.

4 servings. Each serving equals 1 fruit portion.

Calories	67	Cholesterol	0 —
Protein	2 gr.	Fiber	1 gr.
Carbohydrate	16 gr.	Sodium	19 mg.
Fat	0 —		

* * *

PEPPER PIE

CRUST:

- ¾ pound ground beef heart
- ¼ teaspoon pepper
- ¼ teaspoon garlic powder
- ¼ cup onions, chopped fine
- 3 tablespoons unprocessed bran
- 2 Wasa Crisps, crushed
- 2 eggs
- ¼ cup green pepper, chopped fine
- 1 tablespoon chili powder

FILLING:

- ½ cup green pepper, chopped
- 3–4 scallions, chopped
- ½ cup mushrooms, sliced
- 6 eggs, well beaten
- Paprika

Mix crust ingredients well and press into a 9-inch pie dish sprayed with Pam Cooking Spray. Bake at 325° for 1 hour. Blot any grease visible on crust with a paper towel. Cool.

In a pan sprayed with Pam Cooking Spray, sauté vegetables until limp. Combine with eggs and pour into crust. Sprinkle with paprika. Bake at 350° for 25 minutes or until eggs are set.

6 servings. Each serving equals 1 protein and ½ cup cooked vegetable portions and ¼ daily bran allowance.

Calories	238	Cholesterol	521 mg.
Protein	27 gr.	Fiber	0.7 gr.
Carbohydrate	7 gr.	Sodium	167 mg.
Fat	11 gr.		

PEACH "ICE CREAM"

1 peach, pitted, peeled and quartered (reserve 2 thin slices for garnish; dip them in lemon juice to prevent darkening)
6 ice cubes
1 tablespoon powdered skim milk
   drop of pure vanilla extract
   drop of almond extract
   Diet Center Lite™ sweetener (or other artificial sweetener) to taste
2 teaspoons fresh lemon or lime juice
   Sprigs of fresh mint or ground cinnamon

Place all ingredients except garnishes in blender and blend until the mixture is smooth and nearly double in volume. Garnish with the reserved peach slices, mint or a sprinkle of cinnamon.

2 servings. Each serving equals ½ fruit portion and daily milk allowance.

Calories	36	Cholesterol	1 mg.
Protein	2 gr.	Fiber	0.3 gr.
Carbohydrate	8 gr.	Sodium	19 mg.
Fat	0 —		

Five Recipes for Using Up the Summer Zucchini

The best way to get all the nutrients in fresh vegetables is to grow them yourself. Gardening also happens to be physically demanding and psychically rewarding. Even if you live in an apartment, there are many herbs that grow *all year round* in a window box or planter. You can even grow strawberries in your living room if you have enough sun.

Fresh fruits and vegetables are among the prime sources of the minerals that chemically aid the body's metabolic processes in absolutely essential ways. Even deficiencies of the so-called trace minerals—the minerals the body uses in infinitesimal amounts—can cause serious illness or death.

Calcium, phosphorus, sodium, chlorine, potassium, magnesium and sulfur are used by the body in the highest concentrations. We call them the macrominerals. Calcium is crucial to healthy bones and teeth, as well as to blood clotting, heart function, digestion, absorption of other nutrients and transmission of nerve impulses. When you are not getting enough dietary calcium, your body takes it from your bones—a cause of bone softening and easy fracture in older people. Vitamin D—the sunshine vitamin—enhances calcium absorption, another good reason to get out in the garden and grow sun-soaked fresh produce.

Iron is probably the best-known of the trace minerals. Iron deficiency is responsible for a common and serious disorder known as anemia. Anemia affects the body's ability to produce the red blood pigment hemoglobin, which carries oxygen from the lungs to the rest of the body. Anemic persons become pale and washed out, feel tired, irritable and depressed. Unchecked anemia can lead to heart tissue impairment, and even changes in brain function and personality.

Dietary supplements of vitamins and minerals can be a good idea for a person who is restricting his intake of foods. But it is not a substitute for eating a *variety* of the freshest produce available. Search out vegetables you haven't had before—the Diet Center Reducing Diet includes more than thirty types of vegetables. Try them all. It's the best way to ensure that you are getting all the vitamins and minerals you need, with the fewest number of calories.

And don't forget, even with all these delicious ways to cook zucchini (one of my favorites), the very best way to get the nutrients—and the taste—in fresh vegetables is to eat them raw.

*
Zucchini Quiche
Zucchini Soup
Chicken with Zucchini and Tomato (M)
Ratatouille Savannah (M)
Zucchini Lasagne (M)
*

ZUCCHINI QUICHE

4   cups zucchini, unpeeled and sliced thinly
½   cup onion, chopped
¼   teaspoon each: parsley, basil, oregano, pepper and
     butter salt
6   eggs, beaten well
⅛   cup nonfat dry milk

Spray pan with Pam Cooking Spray. Cook zucchini, onion, and herbs and spices over medium heat for 10 minutes (should be tender). Spray a 10-inch glass pie pan. Beat eggs with dry milk. Combine with cooked vegetables and bake in oven 15 minutes at 375°.

4 servings. Each serving equals ⅓ protein and ½ cup cooked vegetable portions and daily milk allowance.

Calories	162	Cholesterol	413 mg.
Protein	12 gr.	Fiber	1 gr.
Carbohydrate	10 gr.	Sodium	125 mg.
Fat	8 gr.		

ZUCCHINI SOUP

1½   cups zucchini, sliced, plus 3 paper-thin slices for garnish
½   cup diced onions
½   cup celery
     Salt and pepper to taste
3   leaves of fresh basil, chopped, or ½ teaspoon dried basil
½   cup Homemade Chicken Stock (see page 62)

Put all ingredients in one pot and simmer for 30 minutes. Then remove from heat, put in blender and blend. Serve hot with slices of raw zucchini on top.

2 servings. Each serving equals 1 cup cooked vegetables portion.

Calories	40	Cholesterol	0 —
Protein	2 gr.	Fiber	1.6 gr.
Carbohydrate	9 gr.	Sodium	253 mg.
Fat	0 —		

CHICKEN WITH ZUCCHINI AND TOMATO (M)

1   broiler-fryer chicken, cut into serving pieces
1½   teaspoon salt (optional)
½   teaspoon pepper
½   cup onion, chopped
½   cup fresh parsley, chopped
2   tomatoes, peeled and chopped
1   teaspoon fresh lemon juice
¼   teaspoon dill weed or 1 teaspoon fresh chopped dill
2   zucchini, pared and sliced diagonally

Put chicken in a large skillet, sprayed with Pam Cooking Spray, and sprinkle with 1 teaspoon salt and pepper, then brown on both sides. Add onion and parsley. Cook 5 minutes. Add tomatoes, remaining ½ teaspoon salt, lemon juice and dill weed.

Cover and cook over moderately low heat for 20 minutes. Add zucchini, cover and cook 10 minutes longer or till chicken and zucchini are tender.

4 servings. Each serving equals 1½ protein and ¾ cup cooked vegetable portions.

Calories	346	Cholesterol	197 mg.
Protein	56 gr.	Fiber	1.1 gr.
Carbohydrate	8 gr.	Sodium	158 mg.
Fat	9 gr.		

RATATOUILLE SAVANNAH (M)

2	large cloves garlic, minced
⅓	cup safflower oil
½	teaspoon marjoram
½	teaspoon oregano
¼	teaspoon dill weed or 1 teaspoon fresh chopped dill
1	teaspoon salt (optional) Black pepper, freshly ground Dash of Tabasco sauce
2	large yellow squash, sliced
1	medium eggplant peeled, quartered and sliced
1	cup Bermuda onion, peeled and sliced thin
2	green peppers, sliced in slivers
4	medium-sized firm tomatoes, peeled and sliced

Combine first 8 ingredients, mix well. Let stand 15 minutes to blend flavors. Arrange vegetables in layers in buttered 2½- or 3- quart casserole, beginning and ending with squash. Sprinkle each layer with seasoning mixture before adding another layer. Cover. Bake in preheated oven at 350° for 1 hour. Uncover; sprinkle with freshly ground black pepper. Bake 15 minutes longer. Serve hot or cold.

6 servings. Each serving equals 1-cup portion cooked vegetables and ⅔ daily oil allowance.

Calories	164	Cholesterol	0 —
Protein	3 gr.	Fiber	1.9 gr.
Carbohydrate	12 gr.	Sodium	48 mg.
Fat	13 gr.		

ZUCCHINI LASAGNA (M)

1   pound ground round
    Garlic powder to taste
    Salt, pepper to taste
1   can tomato paste
4   medium tomatoes, chopped, or 1 can water-packed whole
    tomatoes, chopped
    Basil
    Oregano
3   eggs, beaten
2   zucchini, sliced and lightly steamed
1   pound low-fat cottage cheese

Brown beef in pan. Season to taste with garlic powder, salt and pepper. Add tomato paste and tomatoes, season with basil and oregano. Let simmer over low heat about 45 minutes. If sauce becomes too thick, add water. Beat eggs well, add more salt, pepper and garlic powder. Combine eggs and cottage cheese, mixing well. In 9 × 13 baking pan, make a layer of meat sauce, then zucchini, then cottage cheese and eggs; repeat layers, end with a top layer of sauce. Bake in preheated 350° oven for 1 hour. Let set 10 to 15 minutes before serving.

6 servings. Each serving equals 1½ protein and ⅔ cup cooked vegetable portions.

Calories	298	Cholesterol	200 mg.
Protein	30 gr.	Fiber	0.8 gr.
Carbohydrate	12 gr.	Sodium	618 mg.
Fat	14 gr.		

* Fall *

The first crisp days—sweater weather. Change is again in the air. People tend to move in the fall, to change jobs; kids go back to school or leave for college. It can be a very busy time, a time of meetings, commitments and growth. It's a good time to catch up with yourself and take another look at your goals—your diet and health goals, your career goals and, most important, your private goals. Are immediate concerns of daily household or business life swamping you? Are you aware that you have a life above and beyond whatever you are *doing*? Are you remembering to save a few moments to dream . . . for no one ever accomplished something he was too busy (and sometimes that really means too afraid) to dream of—whether it's landing a certain deal, passing an exam or losing those last 10 pounds.

An Autumn Country Sampler

The Diet Center now has more than two thousand franchises; this means we are in every part of the United States as well as in Canada and abroad. As I travel from center to center, meeting all our counselors and many of our dieters, I am impressed time and time again at the richness and variety of traditions represented by this country. A nation of immigrants, we have assimilated foods from all over the world, adapted them to the bountiful natural resources—the abundant meats, fish, fruit, vegetables and herbs—of the New World and made new, highly individual dishes.

At the Diet Center we place a priority on individuality. No diet can be considered effective unless it works for you personally. This is the major reason why the counselors are there—to teach you, but also to learn about you. Every dieter has his or her own pitfalls, moments of the day that are harder than others, emotional low points that are intensely private and can make losing weight extremely difficult.

We want to know your birthday, your anniversary, the day that your child graduates from college. All these occasions are milestones in your life—they are integral parts of the life-progress you call your personal goal. Setting a personal goal is more than saying "I have 22 [or 42 or even 400] pounds to lose." It means becoming the *whole* person you want to be.

For me, losing the nearly 60 pounds I needed to lose was like a dream coming true. Taking what I learned and working with my husband and others to build the Diet Center into what it is today was seeing the American Dream come true. But you don't have to be in business for your hard work to make your dream into reality. All you have to do is commit yourself to start—and keep on starting—from one meal to the next, from one day to the next. Each single successful step brings you closer to the person you want to be. And that is the true meaning of the American Dream—making the most of the opportunity to be the best you can be.

The following dishes are as American as (diet!) apple pie. They're enthusiasm builders too. Enjoy!

*
MENU 1
Tender Baked Chicken
Spicy Okra
Peach Soup with Cinnamon "Dumplings"
*
MENU 2
Cabbage Soup
Chicken Italian Sausage
French Apple Crisp
*
MENU 3
Pepper Steak (M)
Spicy Apple Wheat Germ Muffins (M)
Banana Ice Cream (M)
*

TENDER BAKED CHICKEN

1   *4-ounce chicken breast*
    Juice of one lemon
1   *clove garlic, minced*
    Dash of pepper
1   *tablespoon parsley, chopped*

Remove all skin and fat from chicken. Squeeze lemon over chicken and rub in. Place in a container and cover tightly. Refrigerate 6 to 8 hours or overnight. About 2 hours before serving, sprinkle other ingredients over the chicken. Bake at 325° for 30 minutes. For a crisper surface, turn oven up to 450° for last 5 minutes.

1 serving. Each serving equals 1 protein portion.

Calories	173	Cholesterol	85 mg.
Protein	31 gr.	Fiber	0 —
Carbohydrate	3 gr.	Sodium	74 mg.
Fat	4 gr.		

SPICY OKRA

1½ pounds fresh okra, sliced, or 10-ounce frozen okra,
    thawed and sliced
1 medium onion, chopped
1 clove garlic, minced
1 teaspoon ground coriander
1 teaspoon curry powder
  Freshly ground pepper
2 teaspoons apple cider vinegar or lemon juice

Cook onion and garlic. Add sliced okra, seasonings and vinegar. (If necessary, add small amount of water.) Simmer 15 minutes.

3 servings. Each serving equals 1 cup cooked vegetables.

Calories	32	Cholesterol	0 —
Protein	2 gr.	Fiber	0.7 gr.
Carbohydrate	7 gr.	Sodium	6 mg.
Fat	0 —		

PEACH SOUP WITH CINNAMON "DUMPLINGS"

DOUGH:
4 Wasa Crisps, ground
1 teaspoon Diet Center Lite™ sweetener (or ½ teaspoon
  other artificial sweetener).
½ teaspoon baking powder
½ teaspoon cinnamon
⅛ teaspoon nutmeg
1 egg

(continued)

COBBLER:

  1   *pound peeled fresh peaches (3 cups sliced)*
  ¼ *cup water*
  1   *tablespoon Diet Center Lite™ sweetener (or ½ tablespoon other artificial sweetener).*
  1   *teaspoon cinnamon*

Mix Wasa Crisps, sweetener, baking powder, spices and egg together. Let stand for 3 minutes. Roll dough by hand into ½-inch balls. Place peaches, water, sweetener and cinnamon in a skillet and simmer for 5 minutes. Drop Wasa balls into bubbling peach mixture. Simmer 6 to 10 minutes.

4 servings. Each serving equals ½ bread allowance and ½ fruit allowance.

Calories	108	Cholesterol	69 mg.
Protein	3 gr.	Fiber	1.1 gr.
Carbohydrate	21 gr.	Sodium	79 mg.
Fat	2 gr.		

*   *   *

CABBAGE SOUP

   6   *cups cabbage, chopped*
   1   *medium onion, peeled, sliced and separated into rings*
  ¼ *teaspoon dill weed*
  ¼ *teaspoon caraway seed*
  ⅛ *teaspoon pepper*
 1½ *teaspoons salt (optional)*
   4   *cups hot water*
 12 *tablespoons Diet Center Crunchies (optional)*

Combine all ingredients, cover, simmer 15 to 20 minutes until cabbage and onion are tender.

6 servings. Each serving equals 1 cup cooked vegetable portion and daily Crunchie allowance.

Calories	59	Cholesterol	0 —
Protein	7 gr.	Fiber	0.7 gr.
Carbohydrate	9 gr.	Sodium	142 mg.
Fat	0 —		

CHICKEN ITALIAN SAUSAGE

- 12 4-ounce chicken breasts, ground
- 2 tablespoons chili powder
- 1 large clove garlic, chopped
- 3 teaspoons fennel seed
- ¼ teaspoon celery seed
- ½ teaspoon black pepper
- 1 teaspoon cayenne pepper
- ¼ teaspoon salt
- ½ teaspoon coriander
- ¼ teaspoon jalapeno (optional)
- 2 tablespoons fresh chopped parsley

Mix ingredients in food processor. Form into patties and fry in non-stick skillet.

12 servings. Each serving equals 1 protein portion.

Calories	139	Cholesterol	68 mg.
Protein	25 gr.	Fiber	0.5 gr.
Carbohydrate	1 gr.	Sodium	114 mg.
Fat	3 gr.		

FRENCH APPLE CRISP

      4   large apples
      ½   teaspoon cinnamon
      ¼   teaspoon nutmeg
      1   tablespoon Diet Center Lite™ sweetener (or ½ tablespoon
          artificial sweetener)
      1   cup diet cream soda
      1   package unflavored gelatin
      2   teaspoons vanilla
      2   tablespoons Diet Center Protein Powder, Vanilla
      2   tablespoons nonfat dry milk
      1   Wasa Crisp Fiber Plus, crushed

Peel apples and reserve peelings. Slice apples into 9-inch pie pan. Sprinkle with cinnamon, nutmeg, sweetener. Set aside. Heat soda and add gelatin. Pour heated mixture, apple peelings and vanilla into blender. Blend and pour over apples. Mix together remaining ingredients and sprinkle over top of apple mixture. Bake at 350° for 30 to 40 minutes until tender.

4 servings. Each serving equals 1 fruit portion and daily milk allowance.

Calories	127	Cholesterol	1 mg.
Protein	7 gr.	Fiber	1.8 gr.
Carbohydrate	25 gr.	Sodium	21 mg.
Fat	1 gr.		

* * *

PEPPER STEAK (M)

      1   8-ounce beef heart, boiled or baked, then sliced
      1   onion, sliced, or chopped if preferred
      ½   clove garlic, chopped
          Salt and pepper
      1   cup beef stock (homemade from beef heart)
      1   green pepper, sliced

1 tomato, sliced
2 teaspoons arrowroot
⅛ cup cold water
1 tablespoon soy sauce
    Bean sprouts, rice or whole wheat noodles, steamed or
    boiled

Place beef heart in skillet, add onion and garlic, salt and pepper. Add beef stock. Cover and simmer for 5 minutes. Add green pepper and tomatoes. Cook for 10 minutes. Combine arrowroot, water, soy sauce and stir into meat mixture. Bring to a boil; cook for 5 minutes. Remove garlic, if desired. Serve on hot bean sprouts, rice or whole wheat noodles.

2 servings. Each serving equals 1 protein and 1 cup cooked vegetable portions.

Calories	277	Cholesterol	311 mg.
Protein	40 gr.	Fiber	1.5 gr.
Carbohydrate	14 gr.	Sodium	646 mg.
Fat	7 gr.		

SPICY APPLE WHEAT GERM MUFFINS (M)

1½ cups whole wheat pastry flour
½ cup wheat germ
2 teaspoons baking powder
¼ teaspoon salt
½ teaspoon cinnamon
½ teaspoon nutmeg
2 eggs
⅓ cup honey
¼ cup safflower oil
½ cup skim milk
⅓ cup currants
1 large apple, chopped fine

Measure unsifted flour in bowl and stir in wheat germ, baking powder, salt and spices. In second bowl, beat eggs and blend in honey, oil and skim milk. Add the liquid to the dry ingredients with currants and apple. Mix only until dry ingredients are thoroughly moist. Spoon into muffin tins sprayed with Pam Cooking Spray. Bake at 400° for approximately 20 minutes.

10 muffins. Each serving equals daily whole wheat allowance.

Calories	193	Cholesterol	55 mg.
Protein	5 gr.	Fiber	0.6 gr.
Carbohydrate	29 gr.	Sodium	85 mg.
Fat	8 gr.		

BANANA ICE CREAM (M)

Freeze whole bananas (1 per person), peeled and sliced and put in blender frozen. Add vanilla for flavoring. Blend until consistency of soft ice cream.

1 serving. Each banana serving equals 1 fruit portion.

Calories	110	Cholesterol	0 —
Protein	1 gr.	Fiber	0.6 gr.
Carbohydrate	28 gr.	Sodium	1 mg.
Fat	1 gr.		

Picky Eaters, Pizza and Nutrition

The teen years are a very special time of life. If you were an overweight teenager, no doubt you stored away one or two terrible memories of feeling left out, unattractive, unwanted. If you were a thin teenager whose eating habits have caught up with you, you can still recall what it felt like to feel light and free

—and maybe you can also remember those few fat friends who did not have the dates you had, who might have been fun in school but who were somehow never at the school dances.

Teenagers have a slew of special eating problems that are part of adolescence. They are searching for independence—they eat many, if not most, of their calories away from home. That means they are snackers, eating not at meal times but when the spirit moves them, and not eating home-prepared foods, but whatever happens to be at hand—often junk foods from vending machines and take-out places. They are also at the most sensitive age for peer pressure—boys and girls alike can feel tremendous pressure to fit rigid descriptions of what is attractive physically. And boys and girls both have been known to diet (and exercise) themselves into the dangerous starvation condition of *anorexia nervosa*. Yet it is next to impossible to *tell* a teenager what to do. How can you ensure that a teen eats properly?

One of the best ways to get around the healthy assertiveness of teenagers is to offer choices. Meals that offer familiar favorites reworked in nutritious ways (like the Mexican Pizza and Deviled Eggs below) give teenagers choices they can't go wrong with. As with children, expose teenagers to high-quality foods *and* high-quality information. Teens often pride themselves on athletic prowess (energy, endurance) or on fine points of grooming (clear skin and shiny hair, for instance). The links between the right nutrition and healthy looks are well known. Get them reading and experimenting. It's harder to argue with the mirror than with your mother.

*

Mexican Pizza (Quiche)
Deviled Eggs
Cucumber Salad
"Cheesecake" with Strawberry Topping

*

MEXICAN PIZZA (Quiche)

12 ounces ground beef heart
1 small onion
1 small can green chilies (optional)
2 tablespoons taco seasoning
1 cup French-style green beans, drained
1 cup mushrooms, sliced
3 eggs, beaten
1 cup Homemade Chicken Stock (see page 62)
   Dash of garlic
4 Wasa Crisps, crushed

Brown beef heart, onion, chilies and taco seasoning. Put in bottom of round baking dish. Place green beans and mushrooms over beef heart mixture. Blend in beaten eggs, chicken broth, garlic and crushed Wasa, and pour over vegetables and beef. Bake at 350° for 45 minutes.

4 servings. Each serving equals 1 protein and ½ cup cooked vegetable portions and ½ bread allowance.

Calories	269	Cholesterol	439 mg.
Protein	33 gr.	Fiber	0.9 gr.
Carbohydrate	11 gr.	Sodium	179 mg.
Fat	9 gr.		

DEVILED EGGS

2 hard-boiled eggs
1 tablespoon Sybil's Light Mayonnaise (see page 50)
4 fresh mushrooms, chopped
½ teaspoon dry mustard powder
   Dash of Worcestershire sauce
   Dash of salt and pepper
   Paprika for garnish

Peel and slice eggs in half. Remove yolks. Put yolks into bowl and mash lightly. Add remaining ingredients and mix well. Put mixture back into whites. Sprinkle paprika over top.

1 serving. Each serving equals ⅔ protein portion and daily oil allowance.

Calories	137	Cholesterol	283 mg.
Protein	7 gr.	Fiber	0.2 gr.
Carbohydrate	2 gr.	Sodium	108 mg.
Fat	11 gr.		

CUCUMBER SALAD

      4 to 5   cucumbers
         1   cup cauliflower flowerets
         1   green pepper
       ½   cup onion
         1   cup apple cider vinegar
         2   teaspoons celery seed
         1   teaspoon Diet Center Lite™ sweetener (or ½ teaspoon other artificial sweetener)

Slice all vegetables very, very thin except cauliflower (break into small flowerets). Mix all ingredients together. Put in a large glass bowl. Cover with foil. Refrigerate for a day before using.

4 servings. Each serving equals raw vegetable portion.

Calories	58	Cholesterol	0 —
Protein	3 gr.	Fiber	1.8 gr.
Carbohydrate	14 gr.	Sodium	21 mg.
Fat	1 gr.		

"CHEESECAKE" WITH STRAWBERRY TOPPING

8 ounces tofu, pressed
Diet Center Lite™ sweetener (or other artificial sweetener) to taste
2 teaspoons pure vanilla extract
1½ cups hot club soda with 1 tablespoon lemon juice, heated
2 envelopes unflavored gelatin (dissolved in ⅓ cup water)

Put tofu, sweetener and vanilla in blender. Blend well while slowly pouring in the club soda and lemon juice. Add the gelatin-water mixture. Blend 1 minute. Pour into a 1-quart casserole sprayed with Pam Cooking Spray. Refrigerate 2 hours or up to 3 days. If storing longer than 2 hours, cover tightly with plastic film. Top each serving with 1 or 2 strawberries, thinly sliced.

4 servings. Each serving equals ⅓ protein portion.

Calories	57	Cholesterol	0 —
Protein	8 gr.	Fiber	0.1 gr.
Carbohydrate	3 gr.	Sodium	9 mg.
Fat	2 gr.		

Three Italian Dinners

Many ethnic cuisines offer dishes that are leaner—less fatty —than typical American dishes, simply because they use less meat, or use cheaper cuts of meat, which have less fat. (Ethnic dishes that use cheese can also be high in fat.) Believe it or not, it is fat content that determines the grade, and therefore the price, of meat—the highest in fat being considered the tenderest and tastiest. This is true, however, only if you like the taste and texture of fat, for cheaper cuts are in many ways more flavorful if cooked properly.

But fat alone is not the all-purpose culprit you may be

tempted to believe. Like carbohydrate, it is an essential nutrient; it is the body's most efficient way of storing glycerol—i.e., energy. It's also important to provide insulation and protection for muscles, bones and organs. It's crucial for healthy, supple skin. It's only when you have too much fat—and the wrong kind—that fat becomes a problem. It's a problem because certain types of fats (saturated) lead to buildups of blood cholesterol—which has been linked to serious illness like heart attack and stroke.

The difference between saturated fats and unsaturated fats is in the hydrogen atoms that attach to the fat molecule (fatty acid). When a fatty acid is carrying as many hydrogens as it has room for, it is called "saturated." When it has more than one place open, it's called "polyunsaturated." The good news is that polyunsaturated fats can "grab" hydrogen atoms from saturated fats and unsaturate them. That is why now that you're cutting way down on fats and oils, it's important to pay attention to the types of oils you use. The fats in most vegetable oils (oils that are liquid at room temperature) are polyunsaturated; animal fats (solid at room temperature) are not. All fats, no matter what the source, have the same calorie value—about 9 calories per gram.

The following menus feature boneless, skinless chicken breasts, which are practically fat-free. The preferable polyunsaturated fat comes in the tiny amount of cooking oil or in the salad dressing.

*

MENU 1
Chicken Florentine
Grissini (Breadsticks)
Lemon Chiffon Dessert
*

MENU 2
Chicken Italiano (M)
Stuffed Mushrooms
Watercress Salad with Vinaigrette Dressing
Granita di Caffè

*

MENU 3
Pasta Salad Primavera
Cantaloupe Halves Garnished with Strawberries

*

CHICKEN FLORENTINE

  4   chicken breasts (4 ounces each)
1½ pounds (raw) fresh spinach, or 1 package frozen chopped spinach
  ½ cup celery, diced fine
  2   tablespoons onion, grated
  1   egg beaten
  1   teaspoon fresh ginger, grated
2–3 fresh garlic cloves, minced
  4   Wasa crackers, pulverized
      Dash of pepper to taste
      Paprika, garlic powder

Flatten each chicken breast, drain spinach well.

If using fresh spinach, wash thoroughly *but do not soak:* soaking destroys nutrients. Steam the spinach in a covered pan at medium heat, using just the water clinging to the leaves. Drain by squeezing in paper towel and chop fine in a blender. If using frozen spinach, cook according to directions, drain by squeezing in paper towel.

Combine all ingredients except the chicken and mix well. Place ¼ of mixture on each breast. Roll up and secure with toothpicks. Place in pan that has been sprayed with Pam Cooking Spray. Dust tops with paprika and garlic powder. Bake uncovered at 350° for 35 to 40 minutes.

4 servings. Each serving equals 1 protein and 1 cup cooked vegetable portions and ½ bread allowance.

Calories	241	Cholesterol	154 mg.
Protein	36 gr.	Fiber	0.7 gr.
Carbohydrate	11 gr.	Sodium	181 mg.
Fat	5 gr.		

GRISSINI BREADSTICKS

In Italian, *grissino* is a long, thin roll of bread. This type of bread-stick is about ¼ of an inch thick and never has seeds.

1 serving equals one breadstick. Each serving equals 1 bread allowance.

Calories	19	Cholesterol	0 —
Protein	2 gr.	Fiber	0 —
Carbohydrate	3 gr.	Sodium	0 —
Fat	0 —		

LEMON CHIFFON DESSERT

    1   package unflavored gelatin
    4   teaspoons Diet Center Lite™ sweetener (or 2 teaspoons
        other artificial sweetener)
    5   eggs, separated
    ½   cup water
    ½   cup lemon juice
    1   teaspoon grated lemon peel

In medium saucepan, mix gelatin with 2 teaspoons sweetener, blend in egg yolks beaten with water and lemon juice. Let stand 1 minute. Stir over low heat until gelatin is completely dissolved, about 5 minutes. Add lemon peel. Pour into large bowl and chill, stirring occasionally, until mixture mounds slightly when dropped from spoon. In medium bowl, beat egg whites until soft peaks form, add remaining sweetener and beat until stiff. Fold into gelatin mixture. Turn into individual dishes.

5 servings. Each serving equals ⅓ protein portion.

Calories	90	Cholesterol	275 mg.
Protein	7 gr.	Fiber	0 —
Carbohydrate	3 gr.	Sodium	71 mg.
Fat	6 gr.		

* * *

CHICKEN ITALIANO (M)

8   chicken breasts (4 ounces each)

TOMATO SAUCE
3   tablespoons onion, minced
1   clove garlic, crushed
4   cups sliced tomatoes or 1 large can whole tomatoes, chopped
1   tablespoon parsley, chopped
1   tablespoon Italian herb seasoning
½   teaspoon ground oregano
¼   teaspoon pepper

In deep frying pan sprayed with Pam Cooking Spray, sauté onion and garlic until brown. Add tomatoes, and simmer until sauce is thick enough to coat a spoon evenly. Add parsley and spices and cook for another ten minutes.

In a 4 × 12 covered casserole, layer 4 chicken breasts, spread with ½ sauce. Repeat for second layer. Bake at 325° for one hour.

8 servings. Each serving equals 1 protein portion.

Calories	211	Cholesterol	85 mg.
Protein	33 gr.	Fiber	0.6 gr.
Carbohydrate	11 gr.	Sodium	252 mg.
Fat	4 gr.		

STUFFED MUSHROOMS

 5 *large mushrooms*
⅓ *cup spinach, cooked and drained*
 2 *Wasa Crisps Lite Rye, crushed*
 1 *tablespoon onion, minced*
 2 *tablespoons water*
¼ *teaspoon sage*
    Dash of butter-flavored salt (optional)

Remove mushroom stems. Place mushroom caps in shallow baking dish. Chop stems. Combine stems with all other ingredients to make stuffing. Fill mushroom caps. Bake at 350° for 15 to 20 minutes.

1 serving. Each serving equals 1 cup cooked vegetables portion and 1 bread allowance.

Calories	95	Cholesterol	0 —
Protein	5 gr.	Fiber	1.1 gr.
Carbohydrate	18 gr.	Sodium	140 mg.
Fat	1 gr.		

WATERCRESS SALAD

  ½ cup chopped watercress
  ¼ cup diced celery
  ¼ cup sliced mushrooms
  ¼ cup diced green pepper
  ¼ cup diced cauliflower
  3 sliced radishes
  ¼ cup bean sprouts

Mix all ingredients.

1 serving. Each serving equals raw vegetable portion.

Calories	41	Cholesterol	0 —
Protein	4 gr.	Fiber	1.5 gr.
Carbohydrate	8 gr.	Sodium	62 mg.
Fat	0 —		

VINAIGRETTE DRESSING

  ⅔ cup Homemade Chicken Stock (see page 62)
  ⅓ cup apple cider vinegar
  ½ teaspoon oregano or basil
  ½ teaspoon garlic powder
  1 teaspoon chopped or dried parsley
  ½ teaspoon Diet Center Lite™ sweetener (or ¼ teaspoon
     other artificial sweetener)

Mix together all ingredients; more spices can be added if desired. Toss as much dressing as you like with 2 teaspoons oil for one serving.

12 servings. Each serving equals daily oil allowance.

Calories	81	Cholesterol	0 —
Protein	0 —	Fiber	0 —
Carbohydrate	1 gr.	Sodium	0 —
Fat	1 gr.		

GRANITA DI CAFFÈ

  1   package unflavored gelatin
  ½   cup cold water
 1½   cups hot decaffeinated coffee
  3   packages Diet Center Lite™ sweetener (or 1½ packages
       other artificial sweetener)
  ½   teaspoon vanilla

Soften gelatin in cold water. Dissolve in hot decaffeinated coffee. Add sweetener and vanilla. Chill till syrupy. Beat thickened gelatin until double in volume. Chill until firm.

4 servings. Each serving equals ½ daily coffee allowance.

Calories	7	Cholesterol	0 —
Protein	2 gr.	Fiber	0 —
Carbohydrate	0 —	Sodium	3 mg.
Fat	0 —		

* * *

PASTA SALAD PRIMAVERA

PASTA:
  ½   cup unprocessed bran
  ¼   cup Diet Center Protein Powder, Vanilla
  2   eggs

Blend into dough, either in food processor or by hand. Let rest 10 minutes. Knead and cut with pasta maker. If too sticky, dust with protein powder. Let dry about 10 minutes. Cook in 3 quarts boiling water until dough floats, about 15 seconds. Remove and drain.

Toss with 2 tablespoons Sybil's Light Mayonnaise (see page 50), season with fresh cracked pepper, thyme, basil, garlic powder, little salt and any of your favorite seasonings. Set aside.

This pasta is the only pasta recipe allowed on the reducing diet. On maintenance, you may substitute any whole wheat pasta.

VEGETABLES:
  1   large zucchini, sliced
  1   large yellow squash, sliced
  2   celery stalks, sliced
  ¼   red cabbage, sliced
  4   mushrooms, sliced
  2   green onions, chopped
  3   tablespoons parsley, chopped
  6   asparagus stalks blanched and quartered (set aside tips
        for garnish)
  ½   red bell pepper, sliced (set aside for garnish)
  12   ounces shrimp, peeled and steamed in Homemade
        Chicken Stock (see page 62) seasoned with thyme and
        tarragon. Save broth to thin mayonnaise.
  2   tablespoons Sybil's Light Mayonnaise (see page 50)

Toss vegetables and shrimp with 2 tablespoons Sybil's mayonnaise thinned with reserved chicken broth.

Layer in glass container. Begin with layer of pasta followed by layer of vegetables and shrimp, followed by other half pasta, topped with other half vegetables. Garnish top with red bell pepper and tips of asparagus. Chill for a few hours to allow flavors to blend but serve at room temperature.

4 servings. Each serving equals 1 protein and raw vegetables portion and daily bran, ½ daily protein powder and daily oil allowance.

Calories	335	Cholesterol	282 mg.
Protein	37 gr.	Fiber	2.3 gr.
Carbohydrate	16 gr.	Sodium	300 mg.
Fat	15 gr.		

CANTALOUPE

1 serving. Each ½ melon equals 1 fruit portion.

Calories	74	Cholesterol	0 —
Protein	2 gr.	Fiber	0.9 gr.
Carbohydrate	18 gr.	Sodium	17 mg.
Fat	1 gr.		

Some Slimming Thanksgiving Alternatives

Thanksgiving Day—turkey, gravy, stuffing (and I'm not just referring to the bird!), pumpkin pie. There are relatives, guests, football games on TV. The holiday entertaining season kicks off today. Are you ready?

1. *Have you done all your shopping in advance?* Guests may show up with mincemeat pie, but if you have remembered to put extra apples on the table, you don't have to give in to temptation. (By the way, mincemeat is the *most* fattening of all the traditional tempters: a hefty piece can load you with more than 600 calories.) Overtempted? Eat an apple and drink water while you are preparing your holiday dinner.

2. *Have you done most of your cooking in advance?* Exhausting yourself in the kitchen—and missing out on the family and friends relaxing in the living room—can add up to frustration, anxiety and binging.

3. *Have you offered choices? Is there everything on the table
that you need?* The following menu features some familiar holiday favorites that are perfect for you and fine for everyone else
as well. Make sure there's enough. I find that each year brings
more and more diet-conscious diners to my Thanksgiving table.
But then the first thing almost every family gives thanks for is
everyone's continued good health.

*

Holiday Cranberry Sauce (M)
Stuffing Delight
Vegetable Mold
Mock Pumpkin Pie
*

HOLIDAY CRANBERRY SAUCE (M)

2 cups fresh cranberries
1 orange, peeled and chopped
¼ cup water
1 tablespoon Diet Center Lite™ sweetener (or ½ tablespoon
   other artificial sweetener)
1 cup frozen unsweetened strawberries or raspberries,
   defrosted

Put cranberries, orange, and water in medium saucepan. Simmer until cranberries "pop." Remove from heat. Add sweetener
to taste, plus strawberries or raspberries. Chill and serve.

4 servings. Each serving equals 1 fruit portion.

Calories	63	Cholesterol	0 —
Protein	1 gr.	Fiber	1.1 gr.
Carbohydrate	16 gr.	Sodium	1 mg.
Fat	0 —		

STUFFING DELIGHT

24   *Diet Center Svelte Crackers ground into crumbs*
3   *celery stalks, chopped*
1   *egg*
    Garlic powder to taste
    Poultry seasoning to taste
    Salt and pepper to taste
    Homemade Chicken Stock, to moisten (see page 62)

Mix together all ingredients. Great in chicken or fish, too.

4 servings. Each serving equals 1 daily bread allowance.

Calories	73	Cholesterol	69 mg.
Protein	2 gr.	Fiber	0.1 gr.
Carbohydrate	11 gr.	Sodium	98 mg.
Fat	2 gr.		

VEGETABLE MOLD

1½   *cups water with 1 teaspoon lemon juice*
1   *tablespoon unflavored gelatin*
2   *tablespoons apple cider vinegar*
½ to 1   *teaspoon horseradish*
    Dash of salt
    Diet Center Lite™ sweetener (or other artificial sweetener) to taste
1   *cucumber*
1   *cup cabbage, chopped*

Soften gelatin in ½ cup of water. Heat remaining water to a boil. Combine water, softened gelatin, vinegar, horseradish, salt and sweetener and mix together. Chill until partly set. While it is setting, peel cucumber and cut in paper-thin slices. Arrange slices in the bottom of a ring mold, just enough to cover the bottom. Pour part of the jellied mixture over the cucumbers—just enough to coat them well—and let set. Add remaining cucumber and cabbage to the remaining gelatin, fill mold. Chill until set.

2 servings. Each serving equals raw vegetable portion.

Calories	35	Cholesterol	0 —
Protein	4 gr.	Fiber	0.8 gr.
Carbohydrate	6 gr.	Sodium	15 mg.
Fat	0 —		

MOCK PUMPKIN PIE

- 3 cups cooked yellow squash
- 2 eggs
- 2 tablespoons Diet Center Protein Powder, Vanilla
- ¼ teaspoon baking soda
- 2 tablespoons pumpkin pie spice
- 2 tablespoons Diet Center Lite™ sweetener (or 1 tablespoon other artificial sweetener)
- 2 tablespoons nonfat dry milk
  Water

Combine all ingredients in blender. Pour into pie plate. Bake at 350° for 25 to 30 minutes.

3 servings. Each serving equals ¼ protein and 1 cup cooked vegetable portion and ½ daily milk and ½ daily protein powder allowances.

Calories	127	Cholesterol	184 mg.
Protein	13 gr.	Fiber	1.4 gr.
Carbohydrate	7 gr.	Sodium	415 mg.
Fat	4 gr.		

The Big Apple

Here are five reasons why apples—one of the classic bounties of fall—are my personal favorites while dieting (I eat one *every day*) and why they are built into the Diet Center Program.

1. Apples are almost 85 percent water—that makes them juicy and *filling*.

2. The natural sugars in an apple provide your body with energy—but at a slower, more even rate than refined sugars. You get the energy "up"—but not the low blood sugar "down."

3. The mild acids and pectin in apples are good for digestion and elimination.

4. The fiber in an apple requires extra chewing, increasing the production of saliva and massaging the gums. Unlike the sticky sugar in candies and cakes, the sugar in an apple does not cling to the teeth. Both these things mean healthier teeth, fewer cavities.

5. The total nutritional picture contained in an apple—sugars, fiber, water, vitamins and minerals—add up to an almost perfect food for dieters. It has satisfying sweetness, chewiness and texture—and provides *staying power*.

The following recipes offer apples in a variety of new ways—complete with all the benefits of staying power and flavor. But don't neglect the fresh, raw apple: one of its best traits is its packaging—it's always ready to go. Toss it in a purse, a briefcase, a lunch box. Put one in the glove compartment of your car and have it on your way home from work. It can keep you from breaking down the door—and your own willpower—at the pre-dinner hour.

*

Sweet and Sour Salad
Apple Crunch Omelet
Molded Cabbage-Apple Salad
Spicy Bran Muffins

Granny's Apple Parfaits (M)
Diet Center Apple Butter
Protein Slush
*

SWEET AND SOUR SALAD

SALAD:

    1   cup celery, chopped
    1   large apple with peel, chopped
    3½ ounce chicken breast, chopped

DRESSING:

    2   teaspoons oil
    2   tablespoons apple cider vinegar
    2   packages Diet Center Lite™ sweetener (or 1 package
        other artificial sweetener)
    ½   cup water
        Garlic powder to taste
        Oregano to taste
        Diet Center Nice & Spicy seasoning (optional)

Shake all dressing ingredients together and refrigerate. Add more apple cider vinegar to taste. Mix salad ingredients and add ⅓ portion of dressing.

1 serving. Each serving equals 1 protein, raw vegetable and 1 fruit portion and daily oil allowance.

Calories	431	Cholesterol	85 mg.
Protein	33 gr.	Fiber	3.6 gr.
Carbohydrate	47 gr.	Sodium	229 mg.
Fat	14 gr.		

APPLE CRUNCH OMELET

1   *large egg*
1 or 2 *teaspoons skim milk*
     Pinch of salt
½   *medium apple, cored, pared and diced*
1   *Ak-Mak Cracker, crumbled*

Spray non-stick skillet with Pam Cooking Spray. Beat egg and milk. Add salt, apple and Ak-Mak crumbs and pour into heated skillet. Shake pan back and forth until egg is set. Cook until done. Fold in half and serve.

1 serving. Each serving equals ⅓ protein and ½ fruit portions and 1 bread allowance.

Calories	147	Cholesterol	275 mg.
Protein	7 gr.	Fiber	0.6 gr.
Carbohydrate	15 gr.	Sodium	74 mg.
Fat	6 gr.		

MOLDED CABBAGE-APPLE SALAD

2   *envelopes unflavored gelatin*
3   *cups water, divided into ½ cup and 2½ cups*
⅓   *cup lemon juice*
1½ *teaspoons Diet Center Lite™ sweetener (or ¾ teaspoon other artificial sweetener) or to taste*
⅛   *teaspoon salt (optional)*
2   *tablespoons apple cider vinegar*
2   *medium red apples (1 cut in cubes and 1 sliced thin for garnish)*
1   *tablespoon prepared horseradish*
2   *cups loosely packed shredded cabbage*
½   *cup celery, sliced*

Soften gelatin in ½ cup cold water. Add 2½ cups boiling water, lemon juice, sweetener, salt and vinegar. Pour ⅓ cup mixture into mold sprayed with Pam Cooking Spray. Chill until thickened. Lightly press apple slices, skin down, into gelatin, so pretty pattern shows when unmolded. Chill rest of gelatin mixture until consistency of unbeaten egg whites. Fold in apple cubes, horseradish, cabbage and celery. Place in mold. Chill until set.

4 servings. Each serving equals 1 raw vegetable and ½ fruit allowances.

Calories	71	Cholesterol	0 —
Protein	4 gr.	Fiber	0.9 gr.
Carbohydrate	16 gr.	Sodium	30 mg.
Fat	0 —		

SPICY BRAN MUFFINS

- 2 eggs
- 6 tablespoons water
- 6 tablespoons nonfat dry milk
- 1 teaspoon Diet Center Lite™ sweetener (or ½ teaspoon other artificial sweetener)
- ½ teaspoon cinnamon
- ½ teaspoon vanilla
  Few drops banana flavoring
- 1 apple with peel, cut into cubes
- 16 tablespoons unprocessed bran

Place eggs, water, milk, sweetener, cinnamon and flavorings in blender and blend well. Drop apple cubes into blender and grind. Pour into a bowl and stir in bran. Pour into 8 muffin cups sprayed with Pam Cooking Spray. Bake at 350° for 30 minutes. Refrigerate or freeze leftover muffins.

8 servings. Each serving equals 1 daily bread, daily bran and daily milk allowances.

Calories	75	Cholesterol	70 mg.
Protein	5 gr.	Fiber	1 gr.
Carbohydrate	13 gr.	Sodium	48 mg.
Fat	2 gr.		

GRANNY'S APPLE PARFAITS (M)

1 cup plain low-fat yogurt
  Diet Center Lite™ sweetener to taste
2 teaspoons orange liqueur or extract
¼ teaspoon ground cinnamon
2 Granny Smith apples, cored and diced
½ pint strawberries, hulled and cut in half
1 cup fresh blueberries

Blend together yogurt, sweetener, orange liqueur and cinnamon. Layer diced apples, strawberries and blueberries with yogurt in parfait glasses or dishes. Chill until ready to serve.

5 servings. Each serving equals 1 fruit portion.

Calories	81	Cholesterol	4 mg.
Protein	2 gr.	Fiber	1 gr.
Carbohydrate	17 gr.	Sodium	25 mg.
Fat	1 gr.		

DIET CENTER APPLE BUTTER

2 medium apples, peeled and quartered
½ to ¾ teaspoon cinnamon, or to taste
⅛ teaspoon ground cloves
⅛ teaspoon lemon juice
½ package Diet Center Lite™ sweetener (or other artificial sweetener to taste)

Steam apples until soft. Put in blender and puree. Put in dish or storage bowl and add other ingredients. Cool. Spread on crackers or muffins.

8 servings. Each serving equals ¼ fruit portion.

Calories	22	Cholesterol	0 —
Protein	0 —	Fiber	0.3 gr.
Carbohydrate	6 gr.	Sodium	1 mg.
Fat	0 —		

PROTEIN SLUSH

  1 apple with peel, cut up
  1 cup club soda
  2 tablespoons Diet Center Protein Powder, Vanilla
1½ teaspoons nonfat dry milk
  2 packages Diet Center Lite™ sweetener (or 1 package
     other artificial sweetener)
  1 teaspoon vanilla
     Crushed ice

Blend all ingredients together in a blender.

1 serving. Each serving equals 1 fruit portion and daily milk and daily protein powder allowance.

Calories	165	Cholesterol	1 mg.
Protein	18 gr.	Fiber	1.1 gr.
Carbohydrate	25 gr.	Sodium	19 mg.
Fat	1 gr.		

Three New England Fish Dinners

Part of coping with the holiday season means expecting to be confronted with a lot of food out of the house, and eating as lightly as possible while at home. When it comes to protein, energy, vitamins and minerals, delivered with the absolute minimum of fat, there is no better choice than fish. Choose it as often as you can.

We have written a "maintenance contract" to help dieters keep their commitments to themselves as a myriad of social eating situations begin to tempt them. Many of the features of this contract are good to keep in mind as you approach the holidays (these rules hold for dieters on *all* phases of the Diet Center Program):

1. Weigh yourself every morning (this way you can notice which foods are problematic and adjust right away).

2. Be aware of which foods you personally are better off avoiding.

3. Do not become anxious or upset if you gain a pound or two. Relax and visualize your success.

4. *Eat on Time and on a Schedule.*

5. Be prepared—fix foods ahead of time.

6. Sit down to eat. (Keep this in mind during the holiday shopping season and you won't grab destructive, non-nutritive "treats" while you're on the run.)

7. Limit caffeinated drinks to two a day.

8. Eat dinner before 8 P.M. if possible.

9. Exercise every day.

10. Drink eight glasses of water a day.

*

DINNER 1
Lime Flounder
Spinach
Apple Walnut Crisp
*

DINNER 2
Egg White Fish Soufflé
Lime Mushrooms
Spicy Tangerines (or Oranges)

*
DINNER 3
Seafood Roll (M)
Steamed Spinach with Garlic
Slaw with Vegetables
Orange Sherbet (M)
*

LIME FLOUNDER

4   ounces flounder
    Onion powder
    Black pepper
2   tablespoons lime juice

Spray a non-stick pan with Pam Cooking Spray. Place fish in pan and sprinkle on onion powder to taste. Sprinkle with pepper. Cook over medium heat. As fish cooks, baste with juice. Turn once and let fish simmer until cooked.

1 serving. Each serving equals 1 daily protein portion.

Calories	105	Cholesterol	50 mg.
Protein	20 gr.	Fiber	0 —
Carbohydrate	3 gr.	Sodium	54 mg.
Fat	1 gr.		

SPINACH

1   pound spinach, steamed with ¾ cup water

1 serving. Each serving (1 cup) equals 1 daily cooked vegetable allowance.

Calories	47	Cholesterol	0 —
Protein	6 gr.	Fiber	1.1 gr.
Carbohydrate	7 gr.	Sodium	157 mg.
Fat	1 gr.		

APPLE WALNUT CRISP

1   large apple
2   teaspoons lemon juice
    Diet Center Lite™ sweetener (or other artificial sweetener)
    to taste
    Cinnamon to taste
2   tablespoons Diet Center Protein Powder, Black Walnut
4   Wasa Crisps Diet Lite Rye

Cut apple in half, moisten with lemon juice. Place skin side down in baking dish. Dust with sweetener and cinnamon. Bake at 350° for 35 minutes. Mash baked apple and divide into 4 servings. Spread on Wasa Crisps and sprinkle protein powder on top.

4 servings. Each serving equals ¼ fruit portion and ½ bread and ¼ daily protein powder allowances.

Calories	88	Cholesterol	0 —
Protein	5 gr.	Fiber	0.8 gr.
Carbohydrate	17 gr.	Sodium	21 mg.
Fat	1 gr.		

* * *

EGG WHITE FISH SOUFFLÉ

2   pounds of any white fish (such as haddock or halibut)
½   teaspoon pepper
2   teaspoons onion powder
3   egg whites, beaten stiff
1   tablespoon parsley, minced
3   tablespoons chives, minced
2   drops soy sauce

Pre-heat oven to 425°. Place fillets in a pan coated with Pam Cooking Spray. Sprinkle pepper and onion powder over top. Bake 10 minutes. To beaten egg whites add parsley, chives and soy sauce. Blend gently. Spread over fish and cover loosely. Bake another 10–15 minutes until puffed.

8 servings. Each serving equals 1 protein portion.

Calories	119	Cholesterol	56 mg.
Protein	24 gr.	Fiber	0.1 gr.
Carbohydrate	1 gr.	Sodium	79 mg.
Fat	2 gr.		

LIME MUSHROOMS

- 1 cup mushrooms, sliced
   Black pepper to taste
   Garlic powder to taste
- 2 tablespoons lime juice

Place mushrooms in non-stick pan sprayed with Pam Cooking Spray. Cook mushrooms till almost tender, then sprinkle with black pepper and garlic powder to taste. Add lime juice and reduce heat till completely cooked.

1 serving. Each serving equals 1 cup cooked vegetable.

Calories	30	Cholesterol	0 —
Protein	2 gr.	Fiber	0.6 gr.
Carbohydrate	6 gr.	Sodium	11 mg.
Fat	0 —		

SPICY TANGERINES (OR ORANGES)

- 2 cups water
- 2 one-inch cinnamon sticks
- 6 whole allspice
- 5 whole cloves

1 pound tangerines or oranges, peeled and segmented
1 teaspoon Diet Center Lite™ sweetener (or ½ teaspoon
  other artificial sweetener)

Combine water and spices in 2-quart saucepan. Boil 1 minute.
Turn off heat, skim. Place fruit in pan, let cool to room temperature. Add sweetener and mix well. Refrigerate 4 to 24 hours to
blend flavors. Remove citrus from poaching fluid with a slotted
spoon and serve.

3 servings. Each serving equals 1 fruit portion.

Calories	69	Cholesterol	0 —
Protein	1 gr.	Fiber	1.1 gr.
Carbohydrate	18 gr.	Sodium	3 mg.
Fat	0 —		

* * *

SEAFOOD ROLL (M)

1 flounder fillet (approx. 8 ounces, the wider the better)
¼ cup celery, chopped
¼ cup parsley, chopped
¼ cup scallion tops, chopped
18 Diet Center Onion Svelte Crackers
1 egg
1 teaspoon water
½ pound scallops
  Pinch of saffron, if desired

Spray oven pan with Pam Cooking Spray. Lay flounder in center.
Stir-fry celery, parsley and green onion. Put crackers in blender
to pulverize. Beat egg and add water to egg. Add to vegetables
along with scallops, saffron and ¾ of the cracker crumbs. Mix
thoroughly and carefully spoon mixture onto flounder fillet. Roll
up fillet to make a very large roll and secure with toothpicks.
Gently turn the roll over so filling does not come out. Sprinkle

remaining ¼ of cracker crumbs over top of roll. Bake in pre-heated oven at 375° for 30 to 40 minutes.

4 servings. Each serving equals 1 protein portion and ½ cup cooked vegetable portion and ¾ bread allowance.

Calories	157	Cholesterol	123 mg.
Protein	22 gr.	Fiber	0.2 gr.
Carbohydrate	11 gr.	Sodium	259 mg.
Fat	2 gr.		

SLAW WITH VEGETABLES

- 1   cup green cabbage
- 1   tablespoon red cabbage
- 1   tablespoon green pepper
- 1   tablespoon celery
- 1   tablespoon zucchini
- 1   green onion including top
- 1   tablespoon Sybil's Light Mayonnaise (see page 50)
- 1   teaspoon water
- 1   teaspoon apple cider vinegar
- ¼   teaspoon prepared mustard
- ¼   teaspoon liquid sweetener

Grate green and red cabbage, chop remaining vegetables. Mix dressing ingredients together, add to vegetables at least 1 hour before serving.

1 serving. Each serving equals raw vegetable portion and daily oil allowances.

Calories	125	Cholesterol	17 mg.
Protein	2 gr.	Fiber	0.9 gr.
Carbohydrate	7 gr.	Sodium	104 mg.
Fat	11 gr.		

ORANGE SHERBET (M)

3¼ cups fresh orange juice (8 medium oranges, squeezed)
¼ cup fresh lemon juice
5 packages Diet Center Lite™ sweetener (or 2½ packages other artificial sweetener)

Mix ingredients together. Churn-freeze in ice cream freezer, or chill until not quite hard and beat with electric mixer before serving. Makes 1 quart.

4 servings. Each serving equals 1 fruit portion.

Calories	95	Cholesterol	0 —
Protein	2 gr.	Fiber	0.2 gr.
Carbohydrate	22 gr.	Sodium	2 mg.
Fat	0 —		

Two Hunt Suppers

Just as exercise keeps your proportion of body fat to lean tissue low and healthy, it does the same for animals. Unfortunately, however, most livestock producers are not looking for lean animals. Why not—why wouldn't they prefer lean, healthy animals? Because their animals are sold by the *pound* and their meat is rated and *paid for* by its fat content. The higher the fat content, the more the meat costs. Exactly backward, isn't it?

But happily there are animals that still run wild (read: get a lot of exercise!) like deer and elk. Even the strains of these animals which have been domesticated for meat are still leaner and more nutritious than domestic beef, lamb and pork. They are genetically closer to their wild forebears; they develop less body fat and are generally fed diets closer to the nutritive variety they ate in the wild.

Remember, animal meats are good protein sources but not good fat sources. Choose your daily oil (fat) allowance from polyunsaturated vegetable oils. *Never eat visible animal fat,* and read labels on things like breads and crackers to make sure that they are made with vegetable oils and not animal fats like lard. Skim all soups and stews by refrigerating until fat congeals on top, then spooning off. A trick to speed things up when you're in a hurry is to float a few ice cubes on top of the soup. Fat clings to them and the extra melted water can always be boiled away.

*
SUPPER 1
Rabbit Ragout
Squash Fritters
Cabbage Slaw
Persimmon Whip
*
SUPPER 2
Deer Meat Stew
Creamed Cucumbers
Persimmon Cookies
*

RABBIT RAGOUT

2½   pounds rabbit, trimmed
     Paprika
     Black pepper
     Diet Center Good Stuff Seasoning (optional)
6   sprigs parsley
6   green onions
1   cup celery with leaves, coarsely chopped
3   cups water

Cut rabbit into 6 pieces and place in skillets sprayed with Pam Cooking Spray. Season. Brown over medium heat, then place rabbit in large pot, top with vegetables. Add water, and simmer for 1½ hours or until tender. Discard vegetables and trim meat before serving.

10 servings. Each serving equals 1 protein portion.

Calories	249	Cholesterol	103 mg.
Protein	33 gr.	Fiber	0.1 gr.
Carbohydrate	1 gr.	Sodium	62 mg.
Fat	12 gr.		

SQUASH FRITTERS

 1 cup steamed diced yellow squash, well drained
 1 teaspoon dehydrated onion flakes
 1 teaspoon parsley flakes
 1 egg
 2 Wasa Crisps Diet Lite Rye

In blender combine all ingredients and blend just until squash is finely chopped. Drop by tablespoons onto Pam-sprayed Teflon griddle. Cook over moderate heat until browned on bottom. Turn and cook until top is browned.

1 serving. Each serving equals ⅓ protein and 1 cup cooked vegetable portions and 1 bread allowance.

Calories	182	Cholesterol	275 mg.
Protein	10 gr.	Fiber	1.8 gr.
Carbohydrate	22 gr.	Sodium	397 mg.
Fat	6 gr.		

CABBAGE SLAW

 1 medium head cabbage, chopped
 ¼ cup onion, minced
 1 cup celery, chopped
 1 green pepper, sliced or chopped
 4 tablespoons Sybil's Light Mayonnaise (see page 50)
 ¼ cup Egg Salad Dressing (see page 79)

Combine all ingredients in a large container that can be tightly covered. Toss well, for at least 3 minutes.

4 servings. Each serving equals raw vegetable portion and daily oil allowance.

Calories	133	Cholesterol	51 mg.
Protein	3 gr.	Fiber	0.9 gr.
Carbohydrate	6 gr.	Sodium	132 mg.
Fat	12 gr.		

PERSIMMON WHIP

4	persimmons
2	tablespoons lemon juice
1	package unflavored gelatin
½	cup nonfat dry milk
¼	teaspoon ginger
¼	teaspoon nutmeg
½	teaspoon cinnamon
¼	teaspoon mace
½	cup club soda
2	eggs, separated
	Vanilla
2–4	packages Diet Center Lite™ sweetener (or 1–2 packages other artificial sweetener)

Purée persimmons with lemon juice. Set aside. Thoroughly mix gelatin, dry milk, spices and soda on top of double boiler. Stir in egg yolks and purée. Reserve the egg whites. Cook over boiling water, stirring constantly until gelatin is dissolved. Add vanilla, remove from heat and cool. Chill, stirring occasionally, until mixture mounds slightly when dropped from a spoon. Add sweetener. Beat egg whites until stiff. Beat persimmon mixture until fluffy, then fold egg whites into persimmon mixture.

8 servings. Each serving equals 1 fruit portion and daily milk allowance.

Calories	112	Cholesterol	70 mg.
Protein	6 gr.	Fiber	1.3 gr.
Carbohydrate	20 gr.	Sodium	59 mg.
Fat	2 gr.		

* * *

DEER MEAT STEW

- ½ cup cabbage, chopped
- 1 small green onion
- ½ stalk celery
- ⅓ medium yellow squash
- 1 cup water
- 1 teaspoon poultry seasoning
- ½ teaspoon black pepper
- ½ teaspoon salt (optional)
- 4 ounces deer meat, cooked and chopped

Combine all ingredients, except deer meat, in saucepan. Cover and cook just until vegetables are tender. Don't overcook. Remove from heat, add deer meat. Cover and return to heat and simmer for 10 minutes.

1 serving. Each serving equals 1 protein and 1 cup cooked vegetable portions.

Calories	180	Cholesterol	72 mg.
Protein	25 gr.	Fiber	1.2 gr.
Carbohydrate	9 gr.	Sodium	134 mg.
Fat	5 gr.		

CREAMED CUCUMBERS

    5   cucumbers, sliced paper thin
    2   tablespoons apple cider vinegar
    5   tablespoons Sybil's Light Mayonnaise (see page 50)
    1   teaspoon onion powder or garlic powder
    3   green onions, chopped fine
  ½   teaspoon Diet Center Nice & Spicy seasoning

Mix all ingredients together and refrigerate overnight or until cucumbers are marinated.

5 servings. Each serving equals daily raw vegetable and oil allowances.

Calories	129	Cholesterol	17 mg.
Protein	2 gr.	Fiber	1.1 gr.
Carbohydrate	8 gr.	Sodium	82 mg.
Fat	11 gr.		

PERSIMMON COOKIES

    1   egg
    3   tablespoons nonfat dry milk
    8   tablespoons unprocessed bran
  ½   ripe persimmon, including skin
  ½   teaspoon vanilla
       Dash of salt
       Diet Center Lite™ sweetener (or other artificial sweetener) to taste
  ⅛   teaspoon cinnamon
  ⅛   teaspoon nutmeg
    3   tablespoons water

Place all ingredients except water in a blender and blend until smooth, then add water a little at a time. Dole out by teaspoonfuls on cookie sheet sprayed with Pam Cooking Spray. Bake at 350° for 8 to 10 minutes. Best kept in refrigerator.

7 servings. Each serving of 4 cookies equals daily bran and daily milk allowance.

Calories	34	Cholesterol	40 mg.
Protein	2 gr.	Fiber	0.6 gr.
Carbohydrate	6 gr.	Sodium	19 mg.
Fat	1 gr.		

* Winter *

"Chestnuts roasting on an open fire,
Jack Frost nipping at your nose . . ."

It's interesting that wherever one turns for an image of this happy season, one finds images of food. It's as prevalent as snow and sleighbells. Some people just resign themselves to gaining weight in the winter and taking it off in the spring. It can be hard to exercise and even harder to say no to all the home-baked goodies that start to pop up everywhere. Why fight it?

You know why? Because you've worked too hard, come too far, and being fat is too painful. You've got to fight. And there are more ways to fight than you might think, if you've committed yourself to winning the losing game. The spirit of the season is joy, peace—and commitment. Just as is the spirit of losing and maintaining your weight.

Six "Stick to Your Ribs" Breakfasts for Cold Mornings

Let's talk about grain, which is what most breakfast foods, like breads, muffins and cereals, are made of.

The commonest grain in use in the West is wheat. It is made into flour and used in all types of products from pasta to bread to soup and other products thickened by adding starch. What concerns us is what happens to the kernel of wheat as it is processed into flour.

The kernel is made of three main parts: the germ, the bran and the endosperm. The germ is the tiny part in the center of the kernel; it is the developing spore of a new plant and carries concentrated nutrients to support that new life. Next comes the large endosperm, also a food source for the germ but consisting mainly of starch. Then there is the bran, a protective covering, also rich in nutrients, and a major source of fiber. All three are protected by the husk or chaff—which is broken and cast away during milling.

Until recent times, the bran, germ and endosperm were ground together in flour. This resulted in brownish, textured flour and nutritious, firm-textured bread. However, new processes of flour refinement began to make smoother, whiter flour—flour that was nothing but starchy endosperm. The nutrient deficit that resulted from this was so severe that in this country all white flour products must be "enriched"—certain nutrients must be put back in artificially—or they cannot, by law, be transported across state lines. But "enriching" does not and cannot put back a wide range of nutrients that occur in amounts too small to count on the charts—but which still affect your health.

Today, the best ways of ensuring that you are getting all the nutrients and fiber in grain products is to bake your own and/or insist upon the types of whole-grain breads and crackers that are built into the Diet Center Program. The trend back to old-fashioned breads (flat, whole-grain wafers like Wasa are not just old-fashioned; they go back to medieval and even biblical times) is not a fad. It is much sounder eating than most of us grew up with. Stomach and bowel cancers are much more common today than ever before, and they are linked to the lack of fiber in our diets.

Whole wheat flour can always be used in place of white flour in a recipe, and better still is the straight, unground product— cracked wheat. With its rich, nutty flavor and hearty, chewy texture, cracked wheat is perfect for satisfying cereals and breads.

*

Apple-Bran Pancake
Hot Mulled Country Apple Tea
*
Blueberry Bran Muffins
Scrambled Eggs
*
Quick & Easy Whole Wheat Bread (M)
Cottage Egg Spread (M)
Sandy's Orange Apricot Jam
*
Bran Custard
*
Cracked Wheat Overnighter (M)
Egg Nog
*
Poached Eggs with Curried Chicken Sauce
Wasa Cinnamon Toast
Camomile Tea
*

APPLE-BRAN PANCAKES

    1   egg, well beaten
    2   tablespoons unprocessed bran
    1   Wasa Crisp Lite Rye, crushed

¼   apple, grated
¼   teaspoon vanilla
     Dash of Diet Center Lite™ sweetener (or other artificial
     sweetener to taste)
⅛   teaspoon cinnamon

Combine egg, bran and Wasa Crisp, let soak for 5 minutes. Add remaining ingredients. Spread to sides of an 8-inch non-stick pan sprayed with Pam Cooking Spray. Cook over medium-low heat until golden brown on each side.

1 serving. Each serving equals ⅓ protein, ¼ fruit portions, ½ daily bread allowance and daily bran allowance.

Calories	160	Cholesterol	275 mg.
Protein	8 gr.	Fiber	1.1 gr.
Carbohydrate	20 gr.	Sodium	90 mg.
Fat	5 gr.		

HOT MULLED COUNTRY APPLE TEA

4   cups boiling water
4   apple-flavored herb tea bags
4   cinnamon sticks
6   whole cloves

Boil water, add tea bags, cinnamon sticks and whole cloves; reduce to simmer for 30 minutes. Remove cloves. May serve with cinnamon-stick stirrers.

4 servings. Each serving equals 1 daily herbal tea allowance.

Calories	14	Cholesterol	0 —
Protein	0 —	Fiber	0.8 gr.
Carbohydrate	4 gr.	Sodium	8 mg.
Fat	0 —		

*   *   *

BLUEBERRY BRAN MUFFINS

2   eggs
6   tablespoons water
6   tablespoons nonfat dry milk
1   teaspoon Diet Center Lite™ sweetener (or other artificial
    sweetener)
    Few drops banana flavoring
½   teaspoon cinnamon
½   teaspoon vanilla
1   cup blueberries, fresh or frozen
16 tablespoons unprocessed bran

Place eggs, water, milk, sweetener, spices and flavorings in blender and blend well. Drop apple cubes into blender and grind. Pour in bowl and stir in bran. Pour into 8 muffin cups sprayed with Pam. Bake at 350° for 30 minutes. Refrigerate or freeze leftover muffins.

8 servings. Each serving equals 1 bread, daily bran and daily milk allowance.

Calories	84	Cholesterol	70 mg.
Protein	5 gr.	Fiber	1.3 gr.
Carbohydrate	15 gr.	Sodium	51 mg.
Fat	2 gr.		

SCRAMBLED EGGS

2   eggs
4   tablespoons water
    Dash of garlic powder
    Dash of celery powder
    Dash of onion powder
⅛   teaspoon pepper
⅛   teaspoon parsley flakes
¼   cup fresh mushrooms

¼ cup celery, chopped
¼ cup green pepper, chopped
2 tablespoons green onion, minced

In bowl beat 2 eggs well, add water, garlic powder, celery powder, onion powder, pepper and parsley flakes. Heat nonstick pan sprayed with Pam Cooking Spray, and sauté mushrooms, celery, green pepper and onion. When vegetables are tender, add egg mixture, cook a few minutes and turn.

2 servings. Each serving equals ⅓ protein and ⅓ cup cooked vegetable portions.

Calories	96	Cholesterol	275 mg.
Protein	7 gr.	Fiber	0.7 gr.
Carbohydrate	4 gr.	Sodium	94 mg.
Fat	6 gr.		

* * *

QUICK & EASY WHOLE WHEAT BREAD (M)

3 cups warm water
2 tablespoons yeast (2 packages)
½ cup honey
⅔ cup nonfat dry milk
3⅓ cups whole wheat flour
¼ cup safflower oil
2 teaspoons salt
3–4 cups whole wheat flour

Mix warm water and yeast. Add honey, dry milk and 3⅓ cups whole wheat flour. Set this in a warm place for 15 minutes. Then add 3 cups whole wheat flour, oil and salt. Knead for 10 minutes and add the last cup of flour as needed. Let rise at room temperature until doubled in size. Form into 2 loaves. Bake at 350° for 40 to 50 minutes. Take out of pans to cool.

2 loaves. One loaf yields 18 slices. One slice equals ½ daily whole wheat bread allowance.

Calories	138	Cholesterol	1 mg.
Protein	4 gr.	Fiber	0.1 gr.
Carbohydrate	26 gr.	Sodium	132 mg.
Fat	2 gr.		

COTTAGE EGG SPREAD (M)

1½ cups low-fat cottage cheese
½ teaspoon Worcestershire sauce
¼ teaspoon pepper
¼ teaspoon dry mustard
    Salt to taste
¼ teaspoon marjoram
4–6 drops hot pepper sauce
8 hard-cooked eggs, chopped

Combine cottage cheese in bowl with seasonings, stirring until blended. Stir in eggs. Cover and chill several hours or overnight to blend flavors.

4 servings. Each serving equals 1 protein portion.

Calories	248	Cholesterol	562 mg.
Protein	23 gr.	Fiber	0 —
Carbohydrate	4 gr.	Sodium	483 mg.
Fat	15 gr.		

SANDY'S ORANGE APRICOT JAM

1 orange
1 teaspoon Diet Center Lite™ sweetener
1 can water-packed apricots, drained well

¼ cup hot water (simmering)
1 package unflavored gelatin

Blend orange, sweetener and apricots in blender. Dissolve gelatin in water. Mix and chill.

14 tablespoons. One serving of 1 tablespoon equals daily free allowance.

Calories	17	Cholesterol	0 —
Protein	2 gr.	Fiber	0.1 gr.
Carbohydrate	3 gr.	Sodium	2 mg.
Fat	0 —		

*   *   *

BRAN CUSTARD

1½ teaspoons nonfat dry milk
2 tablespoons unprocessed bran
¼ teaspoon cinnamon
¼ teaspoon nutmeg
1 egg, beaten
¼ cup hot water
1 teaspoon Diet Center Lite™ sweetener

Mix milk, bran, spices and sweetener in custard dish. Add water. Bake at 350° for 30 minutes. Remove from oven, add egg and mix well. Bake at 400° for 15 minutes.

(Microwave directions: Mix milk, bran, spices and sweetener in custard dish. Add water. Microwave on high for 2 minutes. Remove from microwave and pour in 1 beaten egg. Mix well. Microwave on high 1 minute.)

Good hot or cold.

1 serving. Each ½ cup serving equals ⅓ protein portion and daily bran and milk allowances.

Calories	111	Cholesterol	275 mg.
Protein	8 gr.	Fiber	0.8 gr.
Carbohydrate	7 gr.	Sodium	89 mg.
Fat	6 gr.		

* * *

CRACKED WHEAT OVERNIGHTER (M)

1 cup cracked wheat
3 cups water
⅛ teaspoon salt
Diet Center Lite™ sweetener (or other artificial sweetener) to taste
2 tablespoons skim milk

In a slow cooker, mix cracked wheat, water and salt. Put the cooker on low heat. Cook all night. Add sweetener and skim milk. Makes 2 cups.

4 servings. Each ½ cup serving equals whole-grain cereal allowance.

Calories	150	Cholesterol	0 —
Protein	5 gr.	Fiber	0.7 gr.
Carbohydrate	32 gr.	Sodium	74 mg.
Fat	1 gr.		

EGG NOG

3 raw eggs
½ teaspoon vanilla
1½ teaspoons nonfat dry milk
½ teaspoon Diet Center Lite™ sweetener (or ¼ teaspoon other artificial sweetener)
Nutmeg
6 ice cubes

Blend all ingredients in blender until ice is melted. Pour into a glass and sprinkle nutmeg on top.

1 serving. Each serving equals 1 protein portion and daily milk allowance.

Calories	251	Cholesterol	824 mg.
Protein	20 gr.	Fiber	0 —
Carbohydrate	4 gr.	Sodium	227 mg.
Fat	17 gr.		

* * *

POACHED EGGS WITH CURRIED CHICKEN SAUCE

1½   ounces cooked chicken, chopped
2   tablespoons green onion, chopped
¼   cup celery, chopped fine
¼   cup green pepper, chopped fine
¼   cup mushrooms, sliced
¾   cup Homemade Chicken Stock (see page 62)
1½   teaspoons nonfat dry milk
     Salt to taste
¼   teaspoon garlic powder
1½   teaspoons curry powder
2   tablespoons pimento
     Pepper to taste
2   eggs, poached

Sauté chicken and vegetables until tender in a small amount of water in a skillet sprayed with Pam Cooking Spray. Add Homemade Chicken Stock, nonfat dry milk and seasonings. Stir until blended. Pour over poached eggs.

2 servings. Each serving equals ⅓ protein and ½ cup cooked vegetable portion and daily milk allowance.

Calories	142	Cholesterol	293 mg.
Protein	14 gr.	Fiber	0.8 gr.
Carbohydrate	6 gr.	Sodium	122 mg.
Fat	6 gr.		

WASA CINNAMON TOAST

   4   *Wasa Crisps Lite Rye*
       Dash cinnamon
       Diet Center Lite™ sweetener (or other artificial sweetener)
       to taste

Run water over Wasa crisps. Sprinkle with cinnamon and sweetener and brown under broiler. Watch closely.

4 servings. Each serving equals ½ bread and ¼ daily oil allowances.

Calories	50	Cholesterol	0 —
Protein	1 gr.	Fiber	0.2 gr.
Carbohydrate	6 gr.	Sodium	0 —
Fat	2 gr.		

Three Cozy Winter Dinners

Now the nights are long, instead of the days. You get up in the dark, and go to work; when you come out of your office it's already dark again. It's (pick one) (A) too cold; (B) too rainy; (C) too depressing to get out and exercise. In many parts of the country, the fresh produce in the markets dwindles to only a few selections. And as if all the food at all those parties weren't bad enough, every year you make a batch of cookies or jam to give as presents. Your friends and family just aren't going to let you out of the kitchen.

Don't let winter get to you. There are lots of ways to get around the worst dieting pitfalls of the season. Begin by taking them *one at a time*.

1. There's nothing you can do about getting up and coming home in the dark, so cross it off your list of gripes. Worry only about those things you can change. It will give you a much stronger, better feeling about your life, because you'll see yourself changing things that can be changed.

2. You can exercise indoors. The Diet Center recommends the mini-trampoline because rebound exercise is aerobic, can be done in front of the TV, or in a hotel room, anywhere. But you can also do other exercises. Buy a video tape and dance along. Music makes exercise go faster and smoother. Try a rowing machine or a stationary bicycle. And don't forget that exercise is really a "good mood insurance policy." If you're doing it every day, you're going to find that things just don't bother you so much.

3. It's true that summer vegetables and fruits are less abundant in the dead of winter. But there are many winter vegetables which deserve attention. Many are yellow vegetables—squashes and roots—and high in vitamin A. And even the trusty old cabbage has its nutritional advantages (vitamin C)—as well as being remarkably versatile and inexpensive. One-half cup of brussels sprouts has as much vitamin C as an orange!

4. You have the willpower to get through the parties but you find your own kitchen incredibly trying. Congratulate yourself on the former and ask why the latter should be so. Might it be that *your own* expectations about what is good and happy at this time of year involve food and cooking? Others will accept what you decide for yourself. If you always bring cookies to the office party, this year bring apples or a vegetable tray. Put your energy into writing more personal cards. It will be appreciated and remembered, and people will respect your dedication to your goals. If you find you must bring a homemade gift, why not put up some jars of Diet Center Apple Butter (page 153) or Sandy's

Orange Apricot Jam (page 178)? Decorate the jars (children are good at this!).

*

DINNER 1
Swedish Meatballs
German Cooked Cabbage
Sliced Radish Salad with Garlic Vinaigrette Dressing (page 56)
Apple Brown Betty
*
DINNER 2
Beef Heart Sausage
Squash Cakes
Apple Rhubarb Bake
*
DINNER 3
Stuffed Cabbage Leaves
Watercress Salad (page 146) with Tangy Basil Dressing (page 70)
Chocolate Strawberry Cake
*

SWEDISH MEATBALLS

1   pound ground beef heart
1   egg, well beaten
¼   cup onion, chopped fine
2   Wasa Crisps Diet Lite Rye, crushed
1   Wasa Crisp Fiber Plus, crushed
3   Diet Center Onion Sveltes, crushed
3   tablespoons chopped parsley
1   teaspoon salt (optional)
¼   teaspoon pepper
⅛   teaspoon paprika
¼   teaspoon grated lemon rind
½   teaspoon lemon juice
¼   teaspoon nutmeg
⅛   teaspoon allspice
    Water to moisten if needed

BROTH INGREDIENTS:
2 tablespoons *Diet Center Beef Crunchies (optional)*
2 tablespoons *Diet Center Chicken Crunchies (optional)*
  Few drops of soy sauce
  Dash of pepper
1 *bay leaf*
1½ *cups water*

Add egg to ground beef heart. Sauté chopped onion in non-stick pan. Add to beef heart. Add Wasa Crisps, Sveltes and seasonings. Shape into 2-inch balls. Bake on cookie sheet coated with Pam Cooking Spray at 325° for 20–25 minutes until brown.

To make broth, steep crunchies, soy sauce, pepper, bay leaf in boiled water for 10 minutes. Drain Crunchies. Pour over meatballs in a saucepan and simmer for 20 minutes.

4 servings. Each serving equals 1 protein and ½ bread and ½ daily onion allowances.

Calories	285	Cholesterol	379 mg.
Protein	41 gr.	Fiber	0.9 gr.
Carbohydrate	10 gr.	Sodium	219 mg.
Fat	8 gr.		

GERMAN COOKED CABBAGE

3 cups shredded red cabbage
¼ cup apple cider vinegar
1 tart apple, chopped
1 teaspoon cloves

Sauté cabbage until tender in a non-stick pan sprayed with Pam Cooking Spray. Add vinegar, apple and cloves. Simmer 1 hour.

2 servings. Each serving equals 1 cup cooked vegetable and ½ fruit portion.

Calories	90	Cholesterol	0 —
Protein	3 gr.	Fiber	2 gr.
Carbohydrate	22 gr.	Sodium	38 mg.
Fat	1 gr.		

SLICED RADISH SALAD

Slice 5 small radishes per person.

GARLIC VINAIGRETTE DRESSING (SEE PAGE 56)

Calories	8.5	Cholesterol	0 —
Protein	0.5 gr.	Fiber	4 gr.
Carbohydrate	1.8 gr.	Sodium	9 mg.
Fat	1.05 gr.		

APPLE BROWN BETTY

   1 10-ounce peeled Rome Beauty apple
      Peel from apple
   3 Wasa Crisps
      Diet Center Lite™ sweetener (or other artificial sweetener) to taste
  ¼ teaspoon cinnamon
  ⅛ teaspoon nutmeg
      Butter-flavored salt to taste (optional)

Slice apple and steam until soft but still firm. Place in small flat dish (such as Corning Ware au gratin dish). In blender, add apple peel, Wasa Crisps, sweetener, cinnamon, nutmeg and butter-flavored salt. Blend until very fine, then sprinkle over apple and bake at 375° for 20 to 25 minutes.

2 servings. Each serving equals ½ fruit portion and 1 bread allowance.

Calories	126	Cholesterol	0 —
Protein	2 gr.	Fiber	1.7 gr.
Carbohydrate	29 gr.	Sodium	32 mg.
Fat	1 gr.		

* * *

BEEF HEART SAUSAGE

1½ pound ground beef heart
1 teaspoon salt (optional)
½ teaspoon poultry seasoning
1 tablespoon fennel seeds
½ teaspoon sage
   Dash of pepper
   Dash of garlic powder

Mix all ingredients together. Shape into links or patties and broil for 6 minutes on each side.

6 servings. Each serving equals 1 protein portion.

Calories	218	Cholesterol	311 mg.
Protein	36 gr.	Fiber	0.2 gr.
Carbohydrate	2 gr.	Sodium	119 mg.
Fat	7 gr.		

SQUASH CAKES

2 cups raw yellow squash, grated
1 tablespoon onion, grated
1 egg

Beat egg until light and fluffy; mix with grated squash and onion. Drop large tablespoonfuls of squash mixture into pan sprayed with Pam Cooking Spray. Cook on each side until brown.

2 servings. Each serving equals ⅓ protein and 1 cup cooked vegetable portion.

Calories	68	Cholesterol	137 mg.
Protein	5 gr.	Fiber	1.1 gr.
Carbohydrate	6 gr.	Sodium	249 mg.
Fat	3 gr.		

APPLE RHUBARB BAKE

    3 tablespoons unflavored gelatin
   2½ cups club soda
    2 teaspoons vanilla
    2 medium apples with peel, cored and sliced
    2 cups sliced fresh rhubarb
       Diet Center Lite™ sweetener to taste
    1 teaspoon apple pie spice or combination of cinnamon
       and nutmeg

Sprinkle gelatin over 1 cup soda to soften. Combine with remaining soda and vanilla and mix well. Pour into a baking dish. Add apples, rhubarb, sweetener, and spices. Mix well. Bake at 350° for 40 minutes or until fruit is tender.

4 servings. Each serving equals 1 fruit portion.

Calories	71	Cholesterol	0 —
Protein	5 gr.	Fiber	1 gr.
Carbohydrate	13 gr.	Sodium	7 mg.
Fat	0 —		

* * *

STUFFED CABBAGE LEAVES

4 large green cabbage leaves
8 ounces tofu, drained
½ teaspoon soy sauce
4 ounces cooked chicken breast
½ cup spinach
Homemade Chicken Stock (see page 62)

Dip cabbage leaves in boiling water until pliable. Mash tofu with soy sauce. Chop chicken and spinach, and mix with tofu. Divide evenly and roll into cabbage leaves. Secure each roll with a toothpick. Place in pot, cover with Homemade Chicken Stock and simmer 30 minutes.

2 servings. Each serving equals 1 protein and ¼ cup cooked vegetable portion.

Calories	174	Cholesterol	43 mg.
Protein	25 gr.	Fiber	0.4 gr.
Carbohydrate	5 gr.	Sodium	167 mg.
Fat	7 gr.		

CHOCOLATE STRAWBERRY CAKE

2 cups apples, chopped
2 cups fresh or frozen unsweetened strawberries
4 eggs
1 tablespoon vanilla
1 tablespoon chocolate extract (optional)
1 tablespoon strawberry extract (optional)
1 tablespoon Diet Center Lite™ sweetener (or ½ tablespoon other artificial sweetener)
1 cup Diet Center Protein Powder, Chocolate
¼ cup nonfat dry milk
2 teaspoons baking soda
1 cup unprocessed bran

Put first 6 ingredients in food processor or blender and blend well. Pour mixture into a large bowl. Add the remaining dry ingredients and mix with an electric mixer. Spray a 9 × 13 baking pan with Pam Cooking Spray. Pour mixture into pan. Bake at 350° for 40 minutes. Cool and cut into 8 equal servings. Refrigerate or freeze.

8 servings. Each serving equals ⅓ protein and ½ fruit portions and daily bran, daily milk and protein powder allowances.

Calories	166	Cholesterol	138 mg.
Protein	22 gr.	Fiber	1 gr.
Carbohydrate	16 gr.	Sodium	261 mg.
Fat	3 gr.		

Christmas Eve Snacks

It is a common misconception that all between-meal snacking is bad. As a child you were probably told that it would "spoil your appetite," but children cannot fill all their nutritional needs at mealtimes. As an adult, you were told that snacking would make you gain weight. Yet, as with so many things, it's not what you do that's the problem, it's the way you do it.

Far from being a bad habit, the right kind of snacking can keep your blood sugar level even. We have been conditioned to reach for chips, candy, soda—convenience foods that are high in sugar, fat, salt and starch. But reaching for raw vegetables, an apple, or a protein snack at the right time can be the difference between losing weight and uncontrolled binging. Midmorning and late afternoon are both times when dieters run into trouble. Reaching for coffee can just make things worse, for in some people caffeine can cause the blood sugar to rise, stimulating insulin production and ultimately causing the blood sugar level to fall further.

During the holidays there are many late nights. Though it's

best not to eat after 8 P.M., should you run out of resolve, it's much better to choose a snack like the ones below than to reach for a sweet, or for a drink. Alcohol is practically poison to a dieter —it turns off the self-censor that helps you monitor your food choices, and it's metabolized as sugar, so it disrupts your blood sugar level. Many a dieter has reported turning into an "eating monster" after the first few sips of wine—unable to stop wolfing down whatever is around. Remember when you're offered a glass of "cheer," you may not be so cheerful when you look at the scale the next morning!

*

Hot Tofu Dip with Raw Peppers, Cucumbers, Celery, Carrots, etc.
Holiday Dip (M)
Okra Dippers (M)
Crab Stuffed Celery Sticks
Peanut Butter Health Rounds (M)
Gingerbread
Canadian Apple Wine

*

HOT TOFU DIP

- 1½   hot green chilies
- 1   teaspoon Tabasco
- 1   tablespoon soy sauce
- 2–3   tablespoons lemon juice
- 2   tablespoons onions, minced
- 16   ounces tofu, pressed
      Diet Center Good Stuff Seasoning (optional)

Put all ingredients in blender and add about ¾ cup water to reach desired consistency. Use as dip with raw vegetables.

10 servings. Each serving equals ⅕ protein portion.

Calories	36	Cholesterol	0 —
Protein	4 gr.	Fiber	0 —
Carbohydrate	1 gr.	Sodium	126 mg.
Fat	2 gr.		

HOLIDAY DIP (M)

12 ounces low-fat cottage cheese
1 tablespoon chives, chopped
1 tablespoon green pepper, chopped
¼ cup onion, chopped
Pinch of salt and of pepper
½ cup of skim milk
Paprika

Mix all ingredients except skim milk and paprika. Thin with the milk to desired consistency. Sprinkle with paprika. For a smoother dip, purée cottage cheese with 1 to 2 teaspoons skim milk in a blender, then stir in vegetables and seasonings.

25 servings. Each serving equals daily milk allowance.

Calories	14	Cholesterol	1 mg.
Protein	3 gr.	Fiber	0 —
Carbohydrate	1 gr.	Sodium	4 mg.
Fat	0 —		

OKRA DIPPERS (M)

VEGETABLE:
1 pound whole okra

DIP:
¼ cup Sybil's Light Mayonnaise (see page 50)
¾ cup plain yogurt
½ teaspoon garlic powder

½ teaspoon paprika
½ teaspoon Dijon mustard
1 tablespoon oil

Steam okra no more than 2 to 3 minutes. Remove from heat, cool and then refrigerate until lightly chillled. Mix ingredients for dip until evenly blended. Cover and refrigerate until thoroughly chilled. Serve dip in small bowl surrounded by whole okras.

10 servings. Each serving equals ⅔ daily oil allowance.

Calories	60	Cholesterol	8 mg.
Protein	1 gr.	Fiber	0 —
Carbohydrate	1 gr.	Sodium	42 mg.
Fat	6 gr.		

CRAB-STUFFED CELERY STICKS

6 ounces fresh crabmeat
1 tablespoon lemon juice
4 teaspoons Sybil's Light Mayonnaise (see page 50)
8–10 celery stalks, washed and cleaned

Flake crabmeat in bowl, add lemon juice and mayonnaise and stir together. Fill celery stalks with mixture. For variety, top with dried parsley, bean sprouts, radishes or Diet Center Crunchies.

8 servings. Each serving equals ¼ protein and ¼ raw vegetable portion and ¼ daily oil allowance.

Calories	38	Cholesterol	24 mg.
Protein	4 gr.	Fiber	0.1 gr.
Carbohydrate	1 gr.	Sodium	75 mg.
Fat	2 gr.		

PEANUT BUTTER HEALTH ROUNDS (M)

     1   egg, beaten
     1   cup honey
    ¾   cup safflower oil
    ¼   cup water
     1   teaspoon salt
     1   teaspoon vanilla
     3   cups quick-cooking rolled oats
     1   cup whole wheat flour
    ¾   cup wheat germ
     1   cup peanut butter–flavored pieces
    ½   cup sunflower seeds

In bowl combine egg, honey, oil, water, salt and vanilla. In another bowl stir together oats, flour and wheat germ. Add liquid mixture to dry ingredients; mix well. Stir in peanut butter pieces and sunflower seeds. Drop dough from teaspoon onto a cookie sheet sprayed with Pam Cooking Spray. Flatten a little. Bake at 350° for 15 to 20 minutes.

3 dozen. Each round equals 1 whole wheat and ½ daily oil allowance.

Calories	128	Cholesterol	8 mg.
Protein	3 gr.	Fiber	0.2 gr.
Carbohydrate	16 gr.	Sodium	69 mg.
Fat	6 gr.		

GINGERBREAD

     1   cup unprocessed bran
    ¼   cup water
     2   eggs
    ¼   cup nonfat dry milk
     1   cup Diet Center Protein Powder, Black Walnut

3 teaspoons Diet Center Lite™ sweetener (or 1½ teaspoons other artificial sweetener)
½ teaspoon baking soda
½ teaspoon baking powder
1 teaspoon vanilla extract
2 teaspoons cinnamon
1 teaspoon nutmeg
1 teaspoon ginger
1 cup unsweetened applesauce

Mix all ingredients together. Pour into 8×8 pan sprayed with Pam Cooking Spray. Bake in 375° oven for 25 to 30 minutes. Refrigerate or freeze unused portion.

8 servings. Each serving equals ¼ fruit portion and daily bran, daily milk and daily protein powder allowance.

Calories	135	Cholesterol	70 mg.
Protein	20 gr.	Fiber	0.9 gr.
Carbohydrate	13 gr.	Sodium	110 mg.
Fat	2 gr.		

CANADIAN APPLE WINE

4 bags Red Apple Herb Tea
1 quart water, boiling
¼ cup apple cider vinegar

Steep 4 bags Red Apple herb tea in water. Refrigerate overnight. Add ¼ cup apple cider vinegar to cold herb tea, then mix with diet 7-Up or sparkling water and serve chilled.

4 servings. Each serving equals one free allowance of herbal tea.

A New Year's Eve Buffet

The first party of the year is sometimes the biggest; the thing to remember is that you, the host or hostess, don't want to miss it.

The essence of successful holiday entertaining, I have found, is to be able to spend time with my guests. In the end, people have really come to visit with you, not to eat fudge cake. So get out of the kitchen and into a conversation!

You can take for granted that many guests also have specific health needs that require restrictive diets; some are losing weight, some are watching what they eat for other reasons. It is most gracious to offer an abundance of choices so that guests can pick and choose according to what they like and need *without calling attention to themselves*. On my holiday table, there are always two punches, the same color, garnished with slices of lime and strawberries. But one has sugar and one does not. Guests are informed of the difference and can choose for themselves without explanation or apology. The same can be done with alcoholic beverages, or soft drinks and food choices with and without sugar.

All the recipes in this buffet are suitable for dieters in the reducing phase of the Diet Center Program. There are three appetizers, two main dishes—chicken and fish—and two salads. Watch the portion size. You know what you are able to eat; you are responsible for making the right choices.

For dessert, there are crêpes with a variety of fillings. You can choose the dietetic fruit fillings offered below, but you might also want to make fruit cakes or Christmas candy available for guests who want them. *However, you are in control*—a simple fruit salad, perhaps with one or two special additions, like raspberries or pineapple, is always appreciated. This is an elegant meal, and you will love these special festive treats while others select the type of food they wish.

All these recipes can be made ahead of time, with the exception of the fish, which can be prepared up to the point of cooking the night before and popped into the oven just before serving.

*

Peach Daiquiri
Chicken Pâté
Spinach Balls
Mushroom Caviar
Sybil's Light Mayonnaise (page 50)
Spicy Chicken Breasts
Fish Fillets à l'Orange
Spinach Salad
Crêpes with Fresh Fruit
*

PEACH DAIQUIRI

  6 fresh peaches
  ¼ cup lime juice
  2 teaspoons rum extract
  2 packages Diet Center Lite™ sweetener (or 1 package
       other artificial sweetener)
  2 cups chopped ice

Put peaches into blender. Blend till mushy. Add all other ingredients, blend till smooth.

6 servings. Each serving equals 1 fruit portion.

Calories	46	Cholesterol	0 —
Protein	1 gr.	Fiber	0.6 gr.
Carbohydrate	12 gr.	Sodium	0 —
Fat	0 —		

CHICKEN PÂTÉ

1   pound cooked boneless chicken breasts
4   medium celery stalks
4   tablespoons onion, chopped
4   tablespoons Sybil's Light Mayonnaise (see page 50)
    Lemon juice to taste

Blend first three ingredients in food processor until very fine. Fold in mayonnaise and a drop of lemon juice. Chill in serving bowl, serve with Wasa Crisps or other dry crackers, or with fresh-cut raw vegetables. This makes one pint of pâté.

16 servings. Each serving equals ¼ protein portion and ¼ daily oil allowance.

Calories	68	Cholesterol	26 mg.
Protein	8 gr.	Fiber	0 —
Carbohydrate	1 gr.	Sodium	49 mg.
Fat	3 gr.		

SPINACH BALLS

2   pounds fresh spinach (or 2 ten-ounce packages of frozen spinach)
3   cups crushed Wasa Crisp Diet Lite Rye
2   teaspoons poultry seasoning
5   eggs, lightly beaten
1   clove fresh garlic, minced (1 teaspoon garlic powder)
1   teaspoon thyme
½   teaspoon black pepper
1   medium onion, minced

If using fresh spinach, wash thoroughly *but do not soak:* soaking destroys nutrients. Steam the spinach in a covered pan at medium heat using the water clinging to the leaves. Drain and chop fine in a blender. If using frozen spinach, cook according to directions, drain and chop.

Mix remaining ingredients into spinach and chill for fifteen minutes in the refrigerator.

Mold into 1½-inch balls. Place on cookie sheet sprayed with Pam Cooking Spray. Bake at 350° for 20 minutes. Serve warm. These can be frozen and reheated.

40 spinach balls. Each serving of 4 spinach balls equals ⅓ protein and ½ cup cooked vegetable and ½ bread allowance.

Calories	105	Cholesterol	137 mg.
Protein	6 gr.	Fiber	0.9 gr.
Carbohydrate	13 gr.	Sodium	84 mg.
Fat	3 gr.		

MUSHROOM CAVIAR

    1   small onion, chopped fine
    1   tablespoon lemon juice
    ½   pound mushrooms, chopped fine
    ¾   teaspoon Worcestershire Sauce
    2   tablespoons Sybil's Light Mayonnaise (see page 50)
        Salt and pepper to taste

Sauté onion in lemon juice in a non-stick pan. Add mushrooms and sauté 5 minutes or until fairly dry. Add Worcestershire and remove from heat. Add enough mayonnaise to bind, and season with salt and pepper to taste. Mound on serving platter or put into a small crock. Chill well and keep refrigerated until time to serve. Garnish with whole mushroom caps and perhaps a sprinkling of real black caviar, and serve with small Melba rounds.

8 servings. Each serving equals ¼ cup cooked vegetable and ¼ daily oil allowance.

Calories	38	Cholesterol	4 mg.
Protein	1 gr.	Fiber	0.4 gr.
Carbohydrate	3 gr.	Sodium	25 mg.
Fat	3 gr.		

SPICY CHICKEN BREASTS

3	medium garlic cloves, minced
1¼	cup onion, minced
1	teaspoon soy sauce
½	cup water
¼	cup fresh lemon juice
5	teaspoons grated ginger
1	tablespoon ground cumin
1	tablespoon honey (or Diet Center Lite™ sweetener or other artificial sweetener to taste)
	Salt, pepper to taste
10	boneless chicken breasts, 4 ounces each

Pre-heat oven to 350°.

Combine all ingredients except chicken, mix well. Rub chicken thoroughly with mixture but do not marinate. Arrange breasts on baking sheet sprayed with Pam Cooking Spray. Bake until chicken is golden brown (about 40 minutes) and juice runs clear when meat is pierced with a fork. Baste once or twice with the mixture. There is no need to turn the chicken during cooking, and it should be served slightly warmer than room temperature. Cut each breast in half before serving.

20 servings. Each serving equals ½ protein portion.

Calories	92	Cholesterol	43 mg.
Protein	19 gr.	Fiber	0.2 gr.
Carbohydrate	2 gr.	Sodium	57 mg.
Fat	2 gr.		

FISH FILLETS À L'ORANGE

- ½ teaspoon cayenne pepper
- 2 teaspoons minced onion
- 1 pound fillets of sole
- ½ lemon or lime
- ½ orange, diced
- ½ teaspoon orange peel, grated

Sprinkle cayenne and minced onion over fish. Lightly squeeze the lemon or lime on top. Roll fillets and secure with toothpicks. Sprinkle with diced orange and orange peel. Bake at 375° for 15 minutes or until fish flakes easily with a fork.

4 servings. Each serving equals 1 protein portion.

Calories	121	Cholesterol	56 mg.
Protein	23 gr.	Fiber	0.2 gr.
Carbohydrate	3 gr.	Sodium	61 mg.
Fat	2 gr.		

SPINACH SALAD

- 6 hard-boiled eggs
- 4 teaspoons water
- 6 teaspoons apple cider vinegar
- 4 teaspoons lemon juice
  Salt, pepper, onion and garlic powder to taste
- 6 cups fresh spinach, washed and torn into bite-sized pieces
- 1 whole red onion, sliced thin.

Pulverize eggs in blender, then add liquid ingredients and spices until the mixture is creamy. Toss spinach and onion lightly in the dressing. Serve on cold plates.

2 servings. Each serving equals 1 protein and raw vegetable portion.

Calories	317	Cholesterol	824 mg.
Protein	25 gr.	Fiber	1.5 gr.
Carbohydrate	18 gr.	Sodium	339 mg.
Fat	17 gr.		

CRÊPES WITH FRESH FRUIT

2   eggs
2   tablespoons flour or 1 tablespoon Diet Center Protein
    Powder, Vanilla
½   teaspoon cinnamon
1   teaspoon honey or 2 teaspoons Diet Center Lite™
    sweetener or 1 teaspoon other artificial sweetener

Beat eggs well. Add remaining ingredients and mix until smooth. Spray a skillet with Pam Cooking Spray and heat until a drop of water sizzles on pan. Pour in crêpe mixture two tablespoons at a time; shake pan so mixture spreads and cooks evenly. Turn when top of crêpe is dry.

Serve with 1 cup sliced strawberries, or fresh applesauce made from one whole, cored (but not skinned) apple cooked in water with a dash of cinnamon and a dash of honey or sweetener.

1 serving. Each serving equals ⅔ protein and 1 fruit portion and ½ daily protein powder allowance.

Calories	238	Cholesterol	549 mg.
Protein	21 gr.	Fiber	0.7 gr.
Carbohydrate	13 gr.	Sodium	140 mg.
Fat	12 gr.		

Super Sunday

Until recently, men were apt to regard dieting as something only women were interested in—until they landed in the hospital with a heart attack or stroke or perhaps missed the raise or promotion and took a good look at their own health.

Today, the intensity of interest in diet and fitness touches everyone. Men are just as conscious as women of what they eat, how much they exercise and how they look and feel. The chief medical problems afflicting men today are largely linked to obesity (high blood presssure, heart disease, arteriosclerosis, stroke), and major corporations are trying to get their work forces eating right and exercising.

One of the worst problems that overweight men have is exactly the opposite of what most overweight women contend with —a positive self-image. You read me right. The positive self-image of a thin and healthy teenager that most men have (most males are lean and lanky during their protracted late adolescent growth spurt) works against them later, when their adolescent eating habits have caught up with them. They're still eating pretzels and cheeseburgers, drinking beer and other alcoholic beverages, but they're not playing ball anymore—they're often not doing much of anything except sitting, behind a desk or in front of a TV or VCR.

The good news is that once men get some nutrition education they begin to make smart eating choices, and to work out, and they lose weight very quickly. Sometimes it helps to treat dieting like a project—be businesslike about it. Gather all the data you need about the diet that sounds best for you. Can you live with it? Would your doctor approve? Has it really worked for other people? (See *The Diet Center Program* for Dr. Lester Petersen's "How to Select a Weight-Loss Program.") Have a physical, so you can arrive at realistic goals and know what your limitations are. Look at the diet as a contract with consecutive performance deadlines—but also be rational and flexible about what it takes to accomplish something really *important*. Remember that a habit takes 21 days to become established. That's not very long. Keep at it.

And don't be afraid to try cooking for yourself. You are in charge of your diet and your weight-loss progress—why not your kitchen as well? The following recipes combine the convenience and nutritional benefits of all Diet Center recipes; if you've never dieted before, you're in for a pleasant surprise!

*

Chicken 'n' Stuffin'
Sliced Cucumbers with Creamy Sprout Dressing
Wasa Apple Pudding
*
Tofu Lasagna (M)
Romaine with Diet Center Ranch Dressing (M)
Papaya Halves with Lime Wedge
*

CHICKEN 'N' STUFFIN'

    4   ounces of chicken breast
    ¼   teaspoon dried basil
    ¼   teaspoon dried oregano
    ½   cup mushrooms, chopped fine
    2   teaspoons red onion, chopped fine
    1½ teaspoons nonfat dry milk
        Lemon juice

Pound chicken breast till thin. Combine remaining ingredients except lemon juice. Stuff chicken breast and roll up. Secure with toothpicks if needed. Baste with lemon juice. In a baking dish sprayed with Pam Cooking Spray, bake at 350° for 25 minutes.

1 serving. Each serving equals 1 daily protein, ¼ daily cooked vegetable and 1 daily milk allowance.

Calories	190	Cholesterol	86 mg.
Protein	33 gr.	Fiber	0.3 gr.
Carbohydrate	4 gr.	Sodium	99 mg.
Fat	4 gr.		

CREAMY SPROUT DRESSING

1½ cups alfalfa sprouts
2   tablespoons lemon juice or apple cider vinegar
½   cup salad oil
    Salt and pepper to taste
½   teaspoon prepared mustard

Combine all ingredients in blender. Blend until smooth, about 1 minute. Serve on salad or as fruit or vegetable dip.

12 servings. Each serving equals 1 daily oil allowance.

Calories	86	Cholesterol	0 —
Protein	1 gr.	Fiber	0.1 gr.
Carbohydrate	1 gr.	Sodium	1 mg.
Fat	9 gr.		

WASA APPLE PUDDING

1   egg, separated
1   Wasa Crisp Lite Rye, broken into ½-inch pieces
1   Wasa Crisp Lite Rye, crushed fine
    Dash of Diet Center Lite™ sweetener (or other artificial sweetener to taste)
¼   teaspoon almond flavoring
¼   teaspoon lemon juice
¼   apple, grated

Beat egg yolk until thick. Add remaining ingredients except egg white. Beat egg white until stiff, but not dry, and fold into mixture.

Pour into a small baking dish, sprayed with Pam Cooking Spray. Bake at 350° for 35 to 40 minutes or until delicately browned.

1 serving. Each serving equals ⅓ protein and ¼ fruit and 1 bread allowance.

Calories	160	Cholesterol	275 mg.
Protein	8 gr.	Fiber	0.5 gr.
Carbohydrate	18 gr.	Sodium	109 mg.
Fat	6 gr.		

* * *

TOFU LASAGNA (M)

¼–½ pound whole wheat lasagna noodles (8)
½ medium onion, chopped
2 cloves garlic, mashed
2 cups whole tomatoes (1 pound can)
2 cups tomato sauce (1 pound can)
1 teaspoon basil
1 teaspoon oregano
1 cup spinach, steamed and chopped
¼ cup grated parmesan cheese
1 pound tofu, mashed
½ teaspoon nutmeg
   Diet Center Nice 'N Spicy seasoning
   Pepper to taste
8 slices mozzarella cheese

Cook noodles; set aside. Sauté onion and garlic in a non-stick pan sprayed with Pam Cooking Spray. Stir in tomatoes, sauce, basil and oregano. Simmer about ½ hour. Mix spinach, parmesan cheese, tofu, nutmeg, Nice 'N Spicy seasoning and pepper. Layer ⅓ of the noodles in a large casserole and pour ½ tomato sauce on top. Repeat layers twice. Top with mozzarella slices to cover. Bake at 350° for 30 minutes.

5 servings. Each serving equals 1 daily protein and 1 cooked vegetable portion and 1 whole grain allowance.

Calories	353	Cholesterol	44 mg.
Protein	26 gr.	Fiber	1.4 gr.
Carbohydrate	35 gr.	Sodium	1088 mg.
Fat	14 gr.		

DIET CENTER RANCH DRESSING (M)

- ½ cup plain yogurt
- ⅓ cup Sybil's Light Mayonnaise (see page 50)
- 1 tablespoon apple cider vinegar
- 1 small clove garlic, minced
- ¼ teaspoon basil, crushed
- ⅛ teaspoon salt
- ⅛ teaspoon pepper

Mix all ingredients together and refrigerate until chilled.

8 servings. Each serving equals ½ daily oil allowance.

Calories	72	Cholesterol	12 mg.
Protein	1 gr.	Fiber	0 —
Carbohydrate	1 gr.	Sodium	51 mg.
Fat	7 gr.		

ROMAINE

1½ cups. Each serving equals a part of raw vegetables portion.

Calories	15	Cholesterol	0 —
Protein	1 gr.	Fiber	0.6 gr.
Carbohydrate	3 gr.	Sodium	7 mg.
Fat	0 —		

PAPAYA

Each serving of ½ papaya equals 1 fruit portion.

Calories	59	Cholesterol	0 —
Protein	1 gr.	Fiber	1.2 gr.
Carbohydrate	15 gr.	Sodium	5 mg.
Fat	0 —		

A Midmorning
or Midafternoon Tea

Sometime after the first of the year, when the holiday push is over and children are back in school, comes a quiet time. For some it's a sort of letdown after the excitement and company; for some it's a needed rest. For everyone it can be a time of reflection before getting lost in the flood of events that every new year brings.

It's important to take time out and take stock of yourself when you are committed to something as profound as the self-change that dieting entails. The best way to beat stress is to be aware of it; don't let it get ahead of you. Watch for the signs of cynicism and irritability that may mean you are "burning out." Remember to divide your worries between the ones you can do something about and the ones you can't. Give up the ones you can't—and concentrate your energy where you know you can do some good. That leads to a healthy feeling of mastery over life—a feeling that can lead to every kind of accomplishment.

Remember to take your successes as seriously as your mistakes. Reward yourself for losing weight by getting a haircut or buying new clothes. Reward yourself by doing a little exercise when you've gone off your diet. Why? Because even though you ate the wrong thing, you did not give up.

Take the time to share with others—because a new you isn't complete until you're in the context of the people around you.

The following recipes are special snacks (to be served in *small* portions). Take them to the office and give everyone a midmorning "up." Invite a neighbor over. Everyone likes to share good news: you're a succes, start spreading the word!

*

Joe's New York Style Cheesecake
Light Raspberry Bavarian (M)
Apple Snaks
Diet Center Inn Fruit Salad

*

JOE'S NEW YORK STYLE CHEESECAKE

FILLING:

16	oz. tofu, pressed well
3	eggs
1	tablespoon lemon juice
1½	teaspoons vanilla extract
1	teaspoon pineapple extract
6	teaspoons Diet Center Lite™ sweetener (or 3 teaspoons other artificial sweetener)
1½	teaspoons nonfat dry milk

CRUST:

6	Wasa Crisp Fiber Plus
2	teaspoons cinnamon
2	teaspoons Diet Center Lite™ sweetener (or 1 teaspoon other artificial sweetener)
1	teaspoon water
2	teaspoons oil

Blend all filling ingredients on high speed in blender until thick. Pour in bowl and set aside. Crush crust ingredients in blender (don't add water or oil yet). Set aside one tablespoon of crust mixture, then add water and oil and press into bottom of 9-inch pie plate sprayed with Pam Cooking Spray. Pour filling over this, smooth with knife and sprinkle 1 tablespoon of crust mixture over top. Bake at 350° for 30 minutes. Serve plain or top with 1½ cups of your favorite fruit.

8 servings. Each serving equals ⅓ protein portion and ½ daily bread and milk allowance. Note: Add ½ fruit portion if topped with fruit.

Calories	107	Cholesterol	103 mg.
Protein	8 gr.	Fiber	2.2 gr.
Carbohydrate	6 gr.	Sodium	33 mg.
Fat	6 gr.		

LIGHT RASPBERRY BAVARIAN (M)

1   package unflavored gelatin
1   cup boiling water
1   cup ice cubes and skim milk
½   cup part-skim ricotta cheese or low-fat cottage cheese
3   packages Diet Center Lite™ sweetener (or 1½ packages other artificial sweetener)
1   cup fresh or thawed unsweetened raspberries

In blender or food processor, combine gelatin and water; process until dissolved. Fill a 1-cup measure with ice cubes, then add skim milk to the top. Add to gelatin mixture; cover and process on high speed until ice is thoroughly melted. Add ricotta or cottage cheese and sweetener; cover and process until completely smooth and non-grainy. Chill in the refrigerator until set. Then beat until fluffy with an electric mixer. Refrigerate again. Garnish with raspberries.

4 servings. Each serving equals ⅓ protein and ¼ fruit portion.

Calories	70	Cholesterol	5 mg.
Protein	7 gr.	Fiber	1.7 gr.
Carbohydrate	8 gr.	Sodium	132 mg.
Fat	2 gr.		

APPLE SNAKS

4 packages unflavored gelatin
2 cups unsweetened applesauce
¾ cup boiling club soda
1 teaspoon vanilla
1 teaspoon Diet Center Lite™ sweetener (or ½ teaspoon
   other artificial sweetener)
½ teaspoon cinnamon

Sprinkle gelatin in medium bowl over 1 cup applesauce. Stir well. Add boiling soda. Stir thoroughly till gelatin is dissolved. Stir in rest of applesauce and other ingredients. Pour into 8- or 9-inch square pan. Chill till firm. Cut in 1-inch squares. Store in large jar in refrigerator.

4 servings. One-fourth (¼) pan equals ½ fruit portion.

Calories	77	Cholesterol	0 —
Protein	6 gr.	Fiber	0.7 gr.
Carbohydrate	14 gr.	Sodium	9 mg.
Fat	0 —		

DIET CENTER INN FRUIT SALAD

1   cup blueberries, fresh or frozen
1   cup strawberries, fresh or frozen
2   apples, sliced thinly
1   cup honeydew melon balls
1   peach, sliced
1   cup blackberries, fresh or frozen
1   cup raspberries, fresh or frozen
1   orange, sectioned
1   cup cantaloupe balls

Toss fruit together in large bowl. Add 2 cups club soda mixed with 2 teaspoons lemon juice and Diet Center Lite™ sweetener (or other artificial sweetener) to taste.

10 servings. Each serving equals 1 fruit portion.

Calories	70	Cholesterol	0 —
Protein	1 gr.	Fiber	2 gr.
Carbohydrate	17 gr.	Sodium	4 mg.
Fat	1 gr.		

Index

213